THE EDTECH COACHING PRIMER

Supporting Teachers in the Digital Age Classroom

ASHLEY McBRIDE

International Society for Technology in Education
PORTLAND, OREGON • ARLINGTON, VIRGINIA

The Edtech Coaching Primer
Supporting Teachers in the Digital Age Classroom

Ashley McBride

© 2021 International Society for Technology in Education

World rights reserved. No part of this book may be reproduced or transmitted in any form or by any means—electronic, mechanical, photocopying, recording, or by any information storage or retrieval system—without prior written permission from the publisher. Email permissions@iste.org to learn more.

Senior Director of Books and Journals: Colin Murcray
Senior Acquisitions Editor: Valerie Witte
Copy Editor: Angela Wade
Proofreader: Joanna Szabo
Indexer: Wendy Allex
Book Design and Production: Danielle Foster
Cover Design: Christina DeYoung

Library of Congress Cataloging-in-Publication Data

Names: McBride, Ashley, author. | International Society for Technology in Education, issuing body.
Title: The edtech coaching primer : supporting teachers in the digital age classroom / Ashley McBride.
Identifiers: LCCN 2021016306 (print) | LCCN 2021016307 (ebook) | ISBN 9781564849229 (paperback) | ISBN 9781564849205 (epub) | ISBN 9781564849212 (pdf)
Subjects: LCSH: Educational technology. | Teachers—In-service training. | Employees—Coaching of.
Classification: LCC LB1028.3 .M392 2021 (print) | LCC LB1028.3 (ebook) | DDC 371.33—dc23
LC record available at https://lccn.loc.gov/2021016306
LC ebook record available at https://lccn.loc.gov/2021016307

First Edition

ISBN: 9781564849229

Ebook version available

Printed in the United States of America

ISTE® is a registered trademark of the International Society for Technology in Education.

About ISTE

The International Society for Technology in Education (ISTE) is home to a passionate community of global educators who believe in the power of technology to transform teaching and learning, accelerate innovation and solve tough problems in education.

ISTE inspires the creation of solutions and connections that improve opportunities for all learners by delivering: practical guidance, evidence-based professional learning, virtual networks, thought-provoking events and the ISTE Standards. ISTE is also the leading publisher of books focused on technology in education. For more information or to become an ISTE member, visit iste.org. Subscribe to ISTE's YouTube channel and connect with ISTE on Twitter, Facebook and LinkedIn.

Related ISTE Titles

Adventures in Authentic Learning: 21 Step-by-Step Projects From an Edtech Coach, by Kristin Harrington

Transform Learning Through Technology: A Guide to the ISTE Standards for Coaches, by Helen Crompton

To see all books available from ISTE, please visit iste.org/books.

About the Author

Dr. Ashley McBride has spent her career working with students and other educators as a secondary English teacher, instructional technology facilitator, and most recently as the director of technology for Dare County Schools. In her work she has designed and implemented professional learning that supports educators and their understanding of digital teaching and learning practices. Additionally, she has led district-wide initiatives that help promote effective integration of technology for students. McBride is a CoSN Certified Educational Technology Leader and in 2020 earned her doctorate in educational technology from Central Michigan University. She also serves as a board member for the North Carolina Technology in Education Society (NCTIES) and is an adjunct professor in Central Michigan University's Masters in Learning, Design and Technology program. You can connect with her on Twitter through her handle @aplusedtech or through the website **edtechcoachingprimer.com**.

Acknowledgements

The Edtech Coaching Primer is a compilation of lessons learned as a teacher, edtech coach, and director. I would like to thank the administrators who saw my potential to fill each of these roles and provide me the opportunity to learn and grow throughout my career in education. Additionally, I would like to acknowledge my extended professional learning community within ISTE, NCTIES, and my coworkers over the years who have provided me with learning opportunities

Thank you to my professors at Central Michigan University in the Doctorate in Educational Technology program for supporting my research in the areas of professional learning and edtech coaching. Each of you played a special role in my understanding of research and educational technology. Dr. Ray Francis for his willingness to provide support when needed. Dr. Troy Hicks for constantly pushing me to think deeper about what I am researching and sharing. Dr. Mike DeSchryver for pushing me to think differently. Dr. Mingyuan Zhang, whose patience with me as I worked through quantitative data analysis prevented me from giving up on research all together. Dr. Jennifer Weible for sharing her passion for qualitative data analysis. And Dr. Kathryn Dirkin who provided mentoring and support both during and after my time in the DET program.

Thank you to the individuals who contributed vignettes to this book. Your willingness to share your stories with readers makes the ideas that are presented more meaningful and relatable.

Thank you to ISTE for publishing this work. And a big thank-you to Valerie Witte and Emily Reed, who worked with me to make this book better than I could have imagined it to be.

Finally, the biggest thank-you goes to my husband, Robert, and my three kids, Jacob, Dillon, and Abby. You provided me encouragement when I doubted myself, laughter when I was stressed, and time to work quietly with no distractions when I needed it. Without the four of you, I would never have had the courage to take on a project such as this. I love you.

This book is dedicated to my parents, Dean and LouAnn Schmidt.

Your strength, wisdom, and kindness have inspired me to continue striving to do more than I ever thought possible.

Contents

Foreword	x
Introduction	xiii

1 Educational Technology and the Need for Coaching — 1

What Is an Educational Technology Coach?	3
The Current State of Educational Technology Coaching Roles	5
Hiring and Assigning the Edtech Coach	8

2 A Structured Approach to the Technology Coaching Role — 9

Structuring the Role of the Edtech Coach	10
Coaching Approaches	15

3 Creating and Facilitating Impactful Professional Learning — 17

Regularly Scheduling Sessions	19
Focused on Pedagogy	20
Setting a Goal and Planning for Professional Learning	20
Planning PD for a District or School Goal	22
Planning PD for a PLC or Individual Goal	27
Necessary Qualities Within Professional Learning Sessions	31

4 Providing Personalized Support to Teachers — 40

- Research — 41
- Co-Planning — 42
- Modeling — 48
- Co-Teaching — 51
- Data Analysis and Usage — 53

5 Implementing Formal Coaching Cycles — 56

- Popular Coaching Cycles and What Can Be Learned from Them — 57
- Edtech Coaching Cycle — 62

6 Focused Leadership Responsibilities — 72

- Finding a Leadership Niche — 73
- Projects and Programs — 73
- Identifying the Work — 76
- Organizing the Work — 77
- Gathering Feedback — 79

7 Putting It All Together — 81
Let Priorities and Support Services Be Known — 82
Remember the Ten-Minute Rule — 83
Know the Rhythm of the School — 84
Be Transparent with the Schedule — 85
Book Yourself — 86

8 Reflecting and Planning for Personal Growth as a Coach — 88

9 Hiring and Supporting the Edtech Coach — 98
Start with a Job Description — 99
Finding the Right Person — 100
Supporting the Edtech Coach — 100
Evaluations — 103

Conclusion: A Call to Action — 112
Appendix: Planning and Scheduling Templates — 115
References — 120
Index — 122

FOREWORD

"To be honest, before you came, I didn't understand why the district thought they needed to hire a digital learning coach," Kathleen told me years after we first met. She worked in the technology department, and part of her role had been to support staff in their use of technology. "But then you got here, and I watched how you connected with teachers. You spoke their language and it all made sense. Now I can't imagine where our district would be if we didn't have this role!"

Kathleen's initial feelings point to an important question we should all be prepared to answer: Why is the role of an educational technology coach important?

At its core, coaching is about relationships and capacity building. The district's choice to add an educational technology coach to the budget as part of their overall 1:1 plan signaled to teachers the commitment to provide long-term support for implementation. They had a vision that not only led to the purchase of devices, but ensured this investment would result in real change in classrooms through the addition of a support role in the form of a digital learning coach. Coaches pave the way for change in the relationships they foster between principals, teachers and themselves by creating a space for conversations that lead to adjustments in professional practice.

To succeed at change, the educational technology coach and practitioner relationship must be rooted in trust. As an experienced classroom teacher, I understand the incredible pressure teachers place on themselves to provide students with the best, most relevant instruction they can. I also know many teachers feel ill-equipped to implement technology effectively. This vulnerability must be navigated carefully and respectfully. Often, when I initially meet with a teacher, they rush to confess their lack of proficiency with technology, presumably to "prepare me" for all the work I have cut out for me. I quickly dismiss this, reminding them that we both bring knowledge to the table—because it's true. Our work is a cooperative effort to design learning experiences for students. We discuss learning objectives in detail, weaving in technology only when it adds to the lesson. Through experimentation, we find success.

Change happens over time and is furthered with each teacher's success. When technology-integrated lessons are executed effectively, teachers are eager to share these experiences with colleagues. In turn, their peers are encouraged to take risks and employ more innovative approaches to instruction. Widespread change requires relationships between principals, district administrators, teachers, and coaches to ensure district goals remain the focus of coaching efforts. One of the things I enjoy most about the role of tech coach is that it serves as a connection point between what could easily be disconnected roles.

Coaches allow districts to scale and support growth for all staff by providing effective, job-embedded professional learning to promote positive change. Capacity is built as teachers apply their learning more deeply, frequently, and consistently by working with coaches rather than working alone. This collaboration fosters conditions for deep reflection and a cycle of continuous improvement.

As districts increasingly add edtech coaching positions to their staffing budgets, it's important that the purpose of these roles be thoughtfully envisioned. In *The EdTech Coaching Primer*, Ashley McBride lays out a clear framework for structuring the role of an educational technology coach to ensure impact and effectiveness. Grounded in the ISTE Standards for Coaches, the book serves as a practical guide to position the educational technology coach as a change agent. Readers will find actionable strategies and resources edtech coaches can use immediately to empower teachers to reach beyond themselves to engage in new models of learning. McBride offers edtech coaches the key ingredients needed to ensure their work helps to amplify great teaching with the purposeful use of technology.

Jennifer (Jenn) Judkins is the Director of Technology & Innovation at Woburn Public Schools in Massachusetts. She is a former middle and high school science teacher and K–12 tech coach who knows first-hand how technology can extend learning and engage students in ways that challenge them to higher levels of thinking. Jenn is a Google Certified Trainer, Google Innovator #NYC19, Raspberry Pi Certified Educator, MassCUE Pathfinder, and PBS Lead Digital Innovator. As a regular presenter at regional and national conferences, Jenn shares her passion for meaningful integration of digital tools by helping teachers gain confidence and proficiency in their use of technology. She can be found on Twitter @teachingforward and online at **www.teachingforward.net**.

INTRODUCTION

This book was made from a collection of personal experiences and years of research on professional learning, coaching, and instructional supports. Having served in K–12 education as a teacher, edtech coach, and administrator charged with supporting edtech coaches, I have seen the value that this role can bring to a school. Unfortunately, there is inconsistency in what the edtech coach does from state to state, district to district, and in some cases school to school. Even with the ISTE Standards for Coaches providing focus for this role, there is still inconsistency that looms over this job. This book aims to push for more consistency by not only bringing awareness to what educational technology coaches are able to do when they are provided an opportunity to align their work with the ISTE Standards for Coaches but also suggest a structure and actions that can help them meet these standards.

Who Should Read This Book?

Consistency for the educational technology coaching role can only come when state agencies, boards of education, district leadership, school administration, edtech coaches, and teachers share the same vision and understanding of the job and its ability to impact teaching and learning. Without this shared vision, appropriate funding cannot be secured to allow for this position and coaches can find themselves being asked to take on tasks that take away from their ability to fully support teachers and students in an impactful way. This book is written with all of these stakeholders in mind and with the intention to start a conversation about how the educational technology coach can be leveraged to create a positive culture of change in K–12 education. While parts of the book are clearly written for specific individuals, creating a book that can help provide a common vision that all stakeholders can refer to and share ensures a common language and alignment of resources that may not be possible if the book had a singular type of reader.

What Is in This Book?

This book is set up to provide not only a vision of what the edtech coaching role can be but also the resources to support the strategies described within that vision. These resources are available for readers to use in their entirety or to adjust to fit their school's needs as long as Creative Commons Attribution-ShareAlike rules are followed. All resources can be found in their printable version by going to **edtechcoachingprimer.com**.

Even though anyone in need of a specific focused topic or resource could jump directly to that chapter and be provided strategies and resources that are immediately understandable and usable, to gain a holistic view of the coaching role and how each of its four categories work together, the book should be looked at linearly.

- Chapter 1 describes the current state of the edtech coaching role.
- Chapter 2 introduces the suggested structure for the edtech coaching role.
- Chapters 3, 4, 5, and 6 dig into each category of the suggested structure and provide action steps and resources to help implement these activities.
- Chapter 7 provides some quick tips and tricks that will help to alleviate scheduling and job-alignment issues.

- Chapter 8 is designed to help the edtech coach reflect on their current strengths, implementation of the ISTE Standards, and own professional growth plan.
- Chapter 9 offers resources for school and district administrators to be able to hire and support an edtech coach.

All the information, strategies, and resources found in these chapters are built to be flexible and practical in nature while remaining grounded in research and best practices. This allows them to be used in various edtech coaching situations. Whether the coach supports 30 teachers or 130, the materials here should be beneficial in some way to anyone who is an edtech coach, works with an edtech coach, or is thinking about implementing an edtech coach in their school or district.

Getting Started

The first step in implementing the edtech coaching role is to get everyone, especially district and school administrators, on the same page as to what the role is meant to do. While the educational technology coaching structure described in this book is a simple way to visually demonstrate the actionable categories of work for the coach, an infographic does not quite dig deep enough to paint a true picture of what these categories represent and the actions that are intended to be taken within them. One way that I have worked to build a common understanding of this role is to get all stakeholders to think critically and describe what implementing the ISTE Standards for Coaches might look like in action. While this book can help with that conversation, the following activity can also provide a place for exploration too.

ADMINISTRATOR ACTIVITY SLIDES

The following activity can be done with any group of people to help them begin to visualize the role of the edtech coach.

1. Set up seven stations.
   - If the group is able to do this activity face-to-face, each station will need:
     - one of the seven ISTE Standards for Coaches sections
     - seven large sheets of chart paper, one for each station
     - markers
   - If this is a virtual activity, you can find a Google Slides presentation that you can use at **edtechcoachingprimer.com**.
2. Split the large group up into smaller collaborative groups of two to four people (seven groups if possible).
3. Instruct the groups to read through the ISTE Standards and indicators that they were provided and begin brainstorming a list of what these standards look like in action.
4. Set a timer for six to eight minutes and let the groups read and write out their responses on the chart paper.
5. When the timer goes off, have teams rotate and do the same at the next station, where they will add to what was already stated by the prior group.
6. Once all groups have been at every station, ask the whole group to reflect by asking questions, such as:
   - What actions did you see repeated among multiple standards?
   - What supports does this person need to offer to teachers?
   - Do these actions align with the actions our edtech coaches are currently asked to do?

Once administration and educational technology coaches have a clear and shared understanding of the goals for the role, it becomes easier to prevent the common pitfalls that keep the edtech coach from working effectively with their staff. As you read through this book, take note that the ISTE Standards for Coaches are placed throughout. This is to keep these standards at the forefront of the work. Keep in mind that the inclusion of a standard in one place does not mean other standards cannot be met with the same strategy or that this is the only way to meet the standard.

1
Educational Technology and the Need for Coaching

As a teacher, I remember often feeling like I was in over my head. Technology training was provided sporadically on teacher workdays where someone would present a tool or strategy while I often thought, "I really should be grading research papers right now." These sessions were never followed up by anyone with any real, practical solutions for implementing the technology with the curriculum I was charged to teach. I would often decide that it was either not the right time for me to implement that specific resource, or I would try to muddle through the implementation alone, adding anxiety and stress to my already full plate.

Teachers want to be effective, and they want to provide the absolute best they possibly can for their students. Yet they are required to take on more than just the teaching role. Teachers are asked to be curriculum specialists, pedagogy specialists, data experts; provide for the social and emotional well-being of each student; and fill out large amounts of administrative paperwork—often while teaching in overcrowded classrooms. The current culture of education now asks that teachers differentiate, individualize, blend, and personalize learning for their students. They usually have to implement these pedagogical changes after only attending a sit-and-get professional development and without having additional support to help them implement what they just learned in the professional development session.

While technology has changed many aspects of daily life, education is often criticized for not changing practices quickly enough to teach the skills students need to be successful. Schools have been working to keep up with these changes by providing more and more funds dedicated to hardware and software that can be utilized by teachers and students. The Federal Communications Commission has dedicated and guaranteed funding to provide internet access to schools, while state and district budgets have been adjusted to allow for the purchase and refresh of devices. The COVID-19 crisis pushed schools to remote learning and shined a light on inequities and gaps that exist when it comes to technology availability and usage for learning. This is leading many districts to begin planning for 1:1 device initiatives and the purchase of internet hotspots to try to close some of these identified gaps. Over the years, many companies and special interest groups have come out and proclaimed that their revolutionary hardware, software, or web platform will be the catalyst for improving student learning experiences and outcomes. In truth, the most influential factor a school can invest in is the teacher, because the technology alone changes nothing.

Dollar after dollar has been spent on initiatives that focus on the implementation of technology, but many of these past initiatives have failed because the approach taken was to hand teachers new tools while providing little to no training to help them understand how to utilize the tools. The lack of training and support has often resulted in technology usage that mimics the teacher-focused structures, which have proven to be ineffective for the majority of students or result in technology not being used at all. Giving teachers who are already overwhelmed and overworked devices and asking them to figure out how to effectively use these tools themselves often results in the continued use of the "traditional" twentieth century classroom practices being delivered through digital worksheets and video lectures instead of paper worksheets and face-to-face lectures. Even with professional development opportunities, conferences, and social media, the change to student-focused schools has been slow. So the question becomes, How can professional learning be structured to help provide teachers with the support they need?

This question can be answered by looking at the research that has been completed on professional learning. In 2017, the Learning Policy Institute released a meta-analysis of thirty-five professional learning studies that summarize the six elements of professional development that can have a profound impact on teacher practices and classroom environment. These include professional learning that is content-focused, incorporates active learning, supports collaboration, uses models and modeling, provides coaching support, offers an opportunity for feedback and reflection, and is offered over a sustained duration (Matherson & Windle, 2017; Darling-Hammond et al., 2017). A big takeaway from this study is that teachers do not learn to implement new practices in a silo. One-time professional development lectures or presentations are not enough. There is a need for school and teacher growth plans that are personalized and not only embody those professional learning sessions but also provide additional support to take the learning beyond the presentation.

What Is an Educational Technology Coach?

There is only so much time in the school year, and there are a lot of standards and skills that need to be taught during that time. As a classroom teacher, this thought often kept me from trying new things with my students. There was always a fear that I would not get through everything they would need before we had to test and they would move on to the next course ill-prepared for what was to come. This was especially true when it came to technology, because it seemed that when I would try to bring in the computer cart and have the students begin to try a new resource or program, that resource would fail. Either I set it up wrong, or the students found the one flaw that I had overlooked. With only forty minutes to get through the day's tasks and thirty kids to work with at once, any technical failure would bring my whole room to a screeching halt. It was usually easier to put the computers away and go back to traditional teaching activities.

BRINGING ABOUT CHANGE

Channing Bennett, Principal

One of the most challenging tasks as a building leader is to find the staff member or team to help ignite change. As a new administrator, I was tasked with rolling out a new initiative for my school. To become more familiar with the initiative and expectations, a meeting with district leadership was held. The team shared the timeline for implementation, as well as the resources and training that were provided to staff. On paper, everything was well organized and school staff members were provided the technology and professional training to be successful. As I met with more individuals and teams, it became apparent there was resistance to this new program.

A meeting was held between the administrative team and the instructional coaches to identify the challenges and create a plan for the next steps. The team decided to address the concerns with the staff and to hold focus groups to determine if we would move forward. The coaches served as the group facilitators, given the fact that they were more familiar with the staff and the process that led to this decision. As a result of these conversations we discovered that staff felt as though they were not part of the decision-making process, and they were concerned with how the change would create a change in technology use. To address these concerns, it was important to determine the barriers to buy-in and evaluate if we would move forward with this initiative. Once it was determined by the staff that the initiative would ultimately benefit students, we then worked with the instructional support team to build staff capacity to use the new technology. Our instructional coaches partnered with the district technology department to provide professional learning sessions, one-on-one support, and modeling with staff.

Regardless of the intent, we must consider the impact of our choices. As a leader it is important to have a clear vision and to include stakeholders in the process. An edtech coach can be instrumental in garnering feedback and buy-in while also supporting staff in embracing change. It is this collaborative effort that perpetuates a positive receptiveness and culture of change.

A coach can provide support before, during, and after a lesson. Coaches can do this for a single teacher or a PLC while helping provide training and support that can grow the entire school community. Coaches are on-site specialists who can provide differentiated methods of professional learning that allows teachers to feel supported, rather than judged (Meeuwse & Mason, 2018). The use of coaching as a practice has been promoted in K–12 since the early 1980s (Showers & Joyce, 1996). Through the years, providing teachers with a coach has proven to not only transform teacher practices (Campbell & Malkus, 2011) but also to have positive effects on student achievement

(Killion, 2017). Providing a school with an edtech coach who can build, facilitate, and support professional learning can help teachers grow more effectively and quickly than throwing ideas at them and hoping those ideas become realities in their classrooms (Liu et al., 2017; Inan & Lowther, 2010).

The continued utilization of a coach can provide a school the ability to offer their teachers professional learning and structured support that meets all of the best practices identified by the Learning Policy Institute (2017). Professional learning sessions facilitated by the educational technology coach can utilize and model active learning strategies. The coach can ensure these sessions promote the connection of teachers from different PLCs to create collaborations throughout their building—or even outside their building—that may not otherwise happen. They can provide effective modeling within teachers' classrooms, and between professional learning sessions the coach can offer formal coaching cycles that provide teachers feedback and allow for reflection on classroom practices. All of this can be delivered over a sustained time frame, as it should all be embedded in the framework of the educational technology coach's role.

The Current State of Educational Technology Coaching Roles

The increased need for the utilization of educational technology practices has led many colleges to offer masters-level degrees specifically focused on the topic. For some states this degree can earn the educator an additional endorsement that can help them demonstrate certification when applying for an educational technology coaching job. As of January 2020, only eighteen states had endorsements specifically designed for the educational technology coaching role.

Edtech coaches come by many different names. They have been known as digital learning coaches, instructional technology facilitators, eLearning coaches, and technology integration specialists, to name just a few. They also come with different responsibilities and support various numbers of schools and teachers. The lack of clarity in the naming, licensing, and structure of the educational technology coaching role has led to a number of radically different structures being established. The chosen structure for the edtech coach directly impacts how the role can be utilized by teachers and how many teachers have access to the educational technology coach on a regular basis.

TRANSITIONING FROM PART-TIME COACH

Marsha Sirkin, Instructional Technology Facilitator

When I first began as an instructional technology facilitator, my schedule included teaching six classes of students a day in the computer lab. I had three computer labs with desktop computers on tables that were bolted to the floor. Although I was hired as an instructional technology facilitator with the expectation of helping move our students and staff forward in digital teaching and learning, my schedule did not reflect that. I like to refer to the first year as my "buy-in year."

I took that year to learn about my staff, school culture, and student needs. I offered staff development in whole-group settings and through weekly newsletters. It was purely a one-size-fits-all situation. To build trust and entice my administrators, I invited them to my lab regularly to give them an opportunity to witness my teaching styles with students. I made sure that they observed practices where students had choices and opportunities to collaborate within STEAM topics that were very complex compared to what they had done in the very same computer lab in years past.

I used that year for adults in the building to have a sense of wonder with what was quickly becoming the most popular classroom on campus. My newsletters were packed with ideas, resources, and tidbits to help teachers fold tech into their instruction. I would always say, "I wish I could spend more time on this with you, but my schedule this year just doesn't allow it. The newsletter will have to do for now."

By planting the seed that I needed a new schedule, the conversation with my principals began. We began playing around with ideas of bringing in an assistant to help out with the computer lab so that I could be more of a resource to teachers as needed. The next year, we began doing just that. By having another human on my team, I was able to ease my way into classrooms to help transform digital teaching and learning.

My next approach to instructional technology facilitating was more of a catch-and-release situation. With a school so large, I worked with a small group of teachers who were "on the same page" as me. I would begin with, "I have something new I would like you to try," or, "Do you have any great projects you would like me to help you kick up a notch?" My hopes were to start with these friends . . . they would get to talking . . . and then everyone would want a time slot with me.

That wasn't quite how it worked out. I found that there was still a large portion of our staff I was not reaching. I remember one of my first "co-teaching" experiences, where the teacher asked me to come in and help teach (I can't remember the topic). When I arrived, she walked out of the room, not to be found until an hour later. I taught the entire lesson alone. It was fun for the students, but I quickly realized that my implementation and planning needed some tweaking.

I joined a network of other ITFs with the Friday Institute (NCDLCN). During this time, the image of myself changed from one of a facilitator, or fisher, to one of an instructional coach. This network gave me incredible tools for conversation with staff and administration for how to utilize and optimize my role as a change agent in our school. I worked on a framework for coaching to reach more staff and students, and moved away from the one-size-fits-all and catch-and-release situations. This framework included monthly meetings with grade levels to assess needs and plan to work together. Although using this framework helped me reach more staff and coaching experiences, I found that, even at grade levels, my learners were all over the place and had vastly different needs from teacher to teacher.

I decided to move to a more personalized approach with a staff needs assessment. From there I was able to see where everyone's individual point A led to B. Also, in the assessment I asked teachers how they liked to learn new things. Another key piece was asking staff what they felt comfortable in helping other educators learn in digital teaching and learning. This gave me a bigger picture of my staff as a whole, and helped me pinpoint the needs of individuals, small groups, and our entire staff. I was also able to find ways to give my staff leadership opportunities.

My personal growth as a coach has changed to more of a "buffet plan," where I offer personalized learning experiences that involve continuous planning, implementation, reflection, revision, and revisiting. This allows me to move everyone to their own point Bs at a rate that pushes them a little bit beyond, each time expanding their comfort zone. As the leadership chair of our school, I am a part of data and planning meetings. This role helps me directly relate everything I do as an instructional coach to school improvement goals and classroom data. One thing is for sure: change is the only thing that stays the same. My ability to work with teachers on a personal level allows for the professional learning I offer to change with their needs.

Hiring and Assigning the Edtech Coach

When COVID-19 required that schools across the world jump into remote learning, educational technology coaches became an even greater asset to any school or district who already had them as an established support for teachers. They were available to help teachers establish learning management systems (if they had not been established already) and support the transition of face-to-face lessons to online learning experiences. But the availability of these coaches looked different for every school because not every school is set up to have an edtech coach who is completely dedicated to just their teachers. Some coaches support one school, while others support a few, and some support tens or even hundreds of schools.

While funding for this role makes many of the assignment decisions for schools and districts, the best practice for implementation of an edtech coach is to hire with support from a specialized district-level administrator and assign the individual to work exclusively in one school (Kane & Rosenquist, 2018). This ensures the coach is integrated into the school culture while remaining protected from being placed into tasks that are outside the purview of their coaching role. The idea of having a district lead for these school-based positions is to help ensure that the educational technology coaches do not get pulled into daily school-based tasks (such as taking on a partial course load) that will prevent them from focusing on the goals and needs of the school community. Being at one school allows the coach to become a part of the school community, provide individualized and just-in-time support, and better help to identify needs for both teachers and students.

2

A STRUCTURED APPROACH TO THE TECHNOLOGY COACHING ROLE

When I became a first-time edtech coach, one of the things I struggled with was the lack of clarity everyone around me had for my role. While my state had a rubric for my evaluation and I had the ISTE Standards for Coaching to help, it seemed like I was constantly being pulled into tasks that did not truly align with those goals. I felt like I was failing and started to think about how I could create a structure that would focus me on those standards while helping others better understand how I was meant to support the school. That experience, as well as my experience as a district-level leader of edtech coaches, has helped me to find a way to better integrate the educational technology coach into the school culture in order to have the most impact on providing support to administrators, teachers, and students.

This book is written to describe a focused structure for the educational technology coach. This structure is intended to be adaptable and to help associate real-world tasks with the standards that have been established for educational technology coaches by ISTE (2019). Using this structure can help ensure the coach is being utilized to their fullest potential and providing their school with the most effective supports possible.

Structuring the Role of the Edtech Coach

The 2019 ISTE Standards for Coaches define the goals of what the coaching role should be. These standards describe the coach as a:

- Change Agent
- Connected Learner
- Collaborator
- Learning Designer
- Professional Learning Facilitator
- Data-Driven Decision-Maker
- Digital Citizen Advocate

The educational technology coaching structure takes all of the actions described within the ISTE Standards for Coaches and organizes the work within these standards into four major actionable categories on which the educational technology coach's role should be focused:

- Formal Professional Learning
- Personalized Teacher Support
- Formal Coaching Cycles
- Focused Leadership Responsibilities

These four elements should intertwine to provide structure to the role of the educational technology coach while ensuring they are meeting the goals set in the ISTE Standards for Coaches (2019).

STRUCTURING THE ROLE OF THE EDTECH COACH

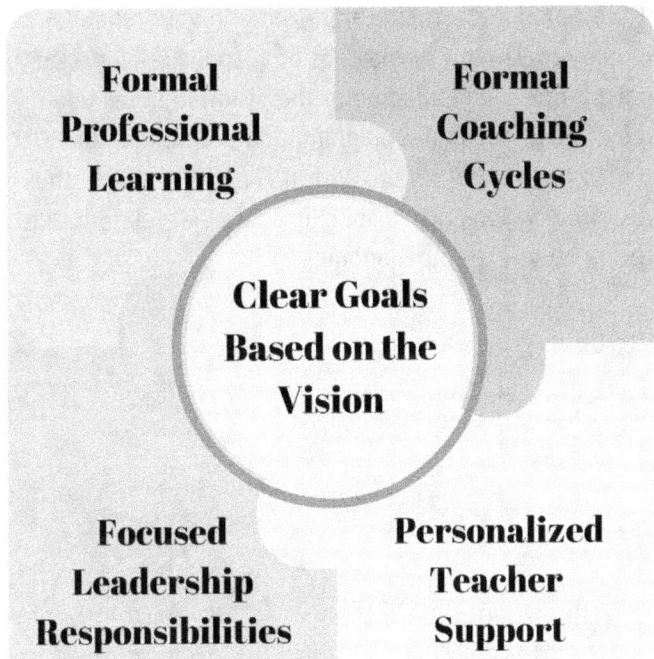

FIGURE 2.1 This image demonstrates how the four elements of the educational technology coach's role come together to focus on the goal(s) set out by the school.

For the structure of the educational technology coaching role to work, school and district leaders need to agree upon a clear vision of what digital teaching and learning should look like in their schools. This clear vision provides coaches a focus that allows them to help their leadership to establish goals and a roadmap to help reach that vision. These goals can be met through the utilization of the four elements of the educational technology coach's role.

Establishing a Vision

The importance of having a vision is described by John G. Gabriel and Paul C. Farmer in their book *How to Help Your School Thrive Without Breaking the Bank*:

> Your school must have a vision that all staff members recognize as a common direction of growth, something that inspires them to be better. An effective vision also announces to parents and students where you are heading and why they should take the trip with you (2009).

The vision is the dream of what teaching and learning can become in your school(s), and while the educational technology coach may or may not be responsible for creating the vision, a coach should have a firm understanding of the vision that has been laid out both by the district and by the school so the planning and programing that is created by the coach is set to help realize that vision. With this understanding, the edtech coach can break the overarching vision up into specific goals that relate to the integration of technology and technology-related pedagogies.

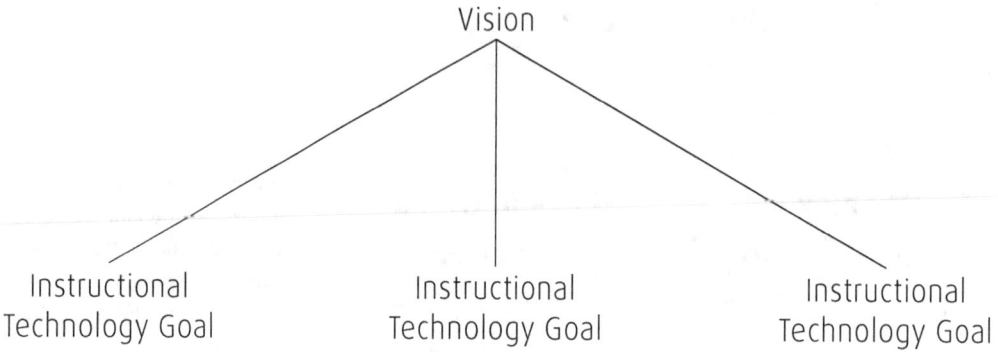

FIGURE 2.2 Break down the vision into achievable and measurable goals.

Formal Professional Learning

With the goals established in response to the vision, the educational technology coach and the administration should establish which of these goals can realistically be worked on throughout the year. Beginning with an understanding of their own current teacher practices and knowledge is essential to make an educated choice about what options for professional learning are best suited for the school and the needs of the staff. The creation of a formal professional learning program that can offer teachers just-in-time professional development focused on their needs and best practices is the easiest place for the educational technology coach to start. Setting aside time and space for these professional learning sessions demonstrates that professional growth and the utilization of digital teaching and learning strategies is a priority of school and district administration. Chapter 3 will discuss in-depth planning practices and considerations for developing a professional learning roadmap that will walk your teachers toward meeting those goals by providing PD on a regular schedule and is based on digital teaching and learning pedagogy, focused on teacher need, and designed to implement active learning strategies.

FIGURE 2.3 Plan out the steps needed to move teachers from where they are to meet the goals that have been established.

Personalized Teacher Support

Because standalone professional development sessions do not provide significant or long-term change in teacher practices, educational technology coaches can provide follow-up support that is focused on the contextual needs of each teacher. This support includes the modeling of best practices, providing teachers with co-planning and co-teaching services, researching strategies and emerging technologies, and offering assistance with data analysis and utilization. Teachers may request these specifically because of their participation in professional learning sessions, the coach may suggest these because of coaching cycle observation and feedback, or administration may suggest these to the teacher as a result of evaluation feedback. Chapter 4 will provide in-depth discussions about these supports and when one might be more beneficial over another.

Formal Coaching Cycles

The use of formal coaching methods can have a profound impact on teacher practices. Often, edtech coaches do not have the opportunity to provide formal coaching cycles because they are inundated with other tasks, are not trained in formal coaching practices, or are not seen as instructional experts but only as technology experts. Educational technology coaches are experts in more than application, software, and hardware use. They are instructional experts who understand strategies that can be more easily implemented because of technology use. By offering a formal coaching cycle, educational technology coaches can observe teachers, offer feedback, and provide personalized support that comes about from the coaching conversations had within the cycle. Chapter 5 looks at the different types of coaching that can be offered, who is a good candidate for coaching, ways to ensure the coaching relationship is a positive one, and resources for determining a coaching cycle that fits the needs of the school community.

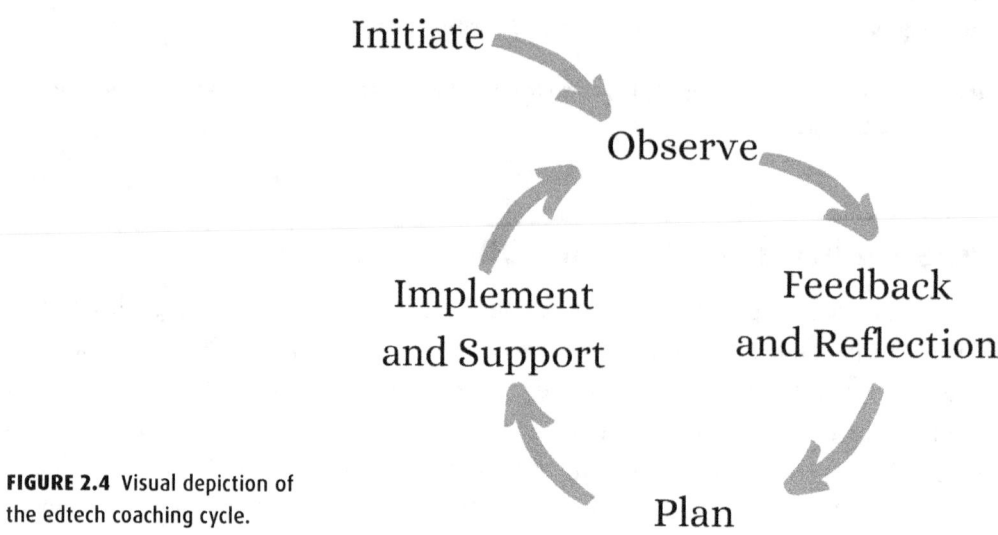

FIGURE 2.4 Visual depiction of the edtech coaching cycle.

Focused Leadership Responsibilities

The educational technology coach is positioned to provide leadership for school or district plans, projects, and programs. Placing too many of these responsibilities on coaches can strain and prevent them from providing the other supports that teachers need. The assignments that are chosen to be placed on coaches should correspond with the types of programs, projects, and plans that may be best suited for the strengths of an educational technology coach. Chapter 6 provides a look at these items and provides strategies for prioritizing the work that the coach performs.

Coaching Approaches

In addition to the ISTE Standards for Coaches (2019), the edtech coaching structure also aligns with a variety of coaching approaches that have been introduced over the years. Some of the most influential coaching literature has been written by Jim Knight and Elena Aguilar. Their respective works each describe three approaches to coaching. While Knight and Aguilar both describe facilitative coaching and directive coaching, they diverge in their third coaching approach.

1. **Facilitative coaching** is an approach that relies on the reflections and insights of the individual being coached. The role of the facilitative coach is not to provide expertise, but to be a reflective partner.

2. **Directive coaching** is an approach that requires the coach to take on the role of master teacher. The coach's job is to impart knowledge and train the individual being coached.

3. **Dialogical coaching** is a marriage of facilitative and directive coaching, where the coach will utilize both reflective questioning strategies while also offering advice where appropriate (Knight, 2018). This partnership allows for teachers to set their own goals, reflect on their practices, be provided suggestions, and participate in the decision-making of which strategies to implement in their practice.

4. **Transformational coaching** looks at coaching the behaviors, beliefs, and being of the individual while also looking at the institution and systems in place surrounding the individual being coached (Aguilar, 2013). This requires the coach not only to guide teachers through their instructional practices, but to dig into the beliefs that influence those actions and break down the barriers within current systems.

The four coaching approaches listed here are only some of the approaches that have been used for educational coaching through the years. Through her research, Cathy A. Toll has determined that there are four categories for coaching approaches (2018). In her work she suggests that coaching approaches usually focus on what the teachers do (behavioral model), what the teachers feel (affective model), what the teachers think (intellectual model), or how teachers work together (collaborative model). The edtech coaching structure is flexible enough to utilize any of these model types depending on the outcome (instructional technology goal) that is established in alignment with the vision.

To further clarify the type of goal that would fall under each of the four models, Table 2.1 is a modified version of a table found in Toll's book, *Educational Coaching: A Partnership for Problem Solving*.

TABLE 2.1 Coaching Models with Example Goals

MODEL	FOCUS	GOAL	EXAMPLE EDTECH COACHING GOAL
Behavioral	What teachers do	Implementation of best practices	Provide teachers the skills and support needed to implement personalized learning with their students.
Affective	How teachers feel	Increased teacher satisfaction and comfort with changes	Provide teachers support as they become more comfortable with the use of technology within their curriculum.
Intellectual	What teachers think	Teacher inquiry, problem-solving, and decision-making	Provide teachers support as they analyze data to determine student gaps and use digital resources to offer differentiated instruction.
Collaborative	How teachers work together	Creation of learning communities	Provide PLCs support in creating shared resources as teachers explore how to integrate the ISTE Standards for Students into their curriculum.

Modified: From *Educational Coaching: A Partnership for Problem Solving* (p. 21) by C. A. Toll, 2018

Original Source: From *Lenses on Literacy Coaching: Conceptualizations, Functions, and Outcomes* (p. 46) by C. A. Toll, 2007, Norwood, MA: Christopher-Gordon

3
CREATING AND FACILITATING IMPACTFUL PROFESSIONAL LEARNING

Technology-focused teacher professional development can come from multiple sources. Outside consultants or professional developers may come into a school to offer PD sessions, a district facilitator may lead a session or series of sessions for teachers, and webinars are readily available from multiple sources. These resources are valuable, and they definitely have their place in the world of teacher professional learning, but these setups usually miss providing effective and personalized follow-up support or the sustained time frame teachers need to be able to make effective long-term changes to their teaching practice. ISTE Coaching Standard 5 describes the educational technology coach as a professional learning facilitator. One of the turning points in my edtech coaching career came when I was able to establish and deliver a structured professional learning program within my school. Through this experience I learned two lessons:

1. Being a daily part of the community where I was providing these learning sessions was a massive benefit.
2. Providing a predictable schedule was important to remaining focused on the growth goals that had been established by my teachers.

As a member of the community, I was able to take all of my observations, impromptu conversations, and daily interactions with teachers and students into account when I went to plan professional learning sessions. I might see that a teacher is relying on slide presentations for content delivery with students, have conversations where the teacher expresses concern that not all of the students are retaining the information they need in order to progress effectively to the next standard or activity, and observe that students are indeed struggling to remain focused during content delivery. These interactions can lead me to adjust my next professional learning session in a way that will model different content delivery methods for the participants. After the session, follow-up conversations, co-planning, modeling, co-teaching, and other support tactics can take what was done in the professional learning session and offer the teacher a less stressful way to implement what was learned within the session itself.

While the edtech coach may help teachers grow through personalized support methods, the creation of a structured professional learning program can promote school-wide growth. Offering teachers a predictable professional learning schedule helps to ensure teachers are given a regular time and space to focus on professional goals and that their learning is a collaborative space that allows them to work, teach, and learn with others from their school community. A school's educational technology coach should be offering regular professional learning sessions that are tailored to the needs of the faculty. These sessions should be active, provide immediately useful strategies and tools that teachers can utilize the next day in their classrooms, and model the type of learning environments that have been proven to better engage students.

Teachers should have time to collaborate with other teachers during these opportunities and be able to solve real classroom problems through those collaborations. Sessions can be delivered in multiple ways. They can be virtual, blended, or face-to-face. Whichever method is chosen, professional development provides a space for teachers to be immersed in learning activities that they may not otherwise have the ability to observe. Now in the place of the learner, teachers can experience the strategies, structures, and activities firsthand, allowing them to realize the impact that these elements can have on the learner, demonstrating that they are capable of building these types of engaging lessons, and showing they have a coach who can help support them as they do it.

Regularly Scheduling Sessions

It is important to make sure that professional development is regularly scheduled and the time provided is protected. This means meetings should happen on a predictable schedule that is set at the beginning of the school year and only changed if absolutely necessary. Providing a regular schedule not only ensures that these meetings happen, but it also demonstrates that a primary focus of the school is the growth of teachers toward realizing the vision that has been established. It also shows that administrators support this professional learning.

When considering a schedule, plan it backward. Determine what goal, based on your established vision, you want to meet and set a realistic timeline for meeting that goal. Think through your individual professional learning topics that need to be explored. While outlining these topics, keep in mind that they need to be timed in a way that helps not only introduce but also dig deep into the concepts that align with your goal. Thinking about the time it will take to really work with teachers on these topics will help you to decide if each topic needs only one session or multiple. Once you have thought through these pieces, ask yourself:

- How often do we want professional learning sessions to happen?
- How long should the average session last?
- What time in our schedules do we already have set aside for such activities?

The schedule that is chosen is dependent upon a number of factors, including school/teacher schedules, needed frequency of the meetings, and the amount of time able to be allotted for each meeting.

Focused on Pedagogy

One of the common misconceptions about educational technology professional development is that it should be focused on a specific web resource, hardware, or software. While there is a place for sessions that explain the use of a particular technology tool, the true goal of educational technology professional development should be on structures, strategies, and active learning processes that can change the learning experience from teacher-centered to student-centered. During these pedagogy-focused professional learning sessions, participants can be exposed to multiple digital resources that can help make differentiated, individualized, blended, and personalized learning environments easier to manage.

Liz Kolb demonstrates the need for technology to be paired with high-leverage learning strategies in her book *Learning First, Technology Second: The Educator's Guide to Designing Authentic Lessons*, where she explains how to use her Triple E Framework to adjust strategies used with digital resources in order to ensure that students are engaged in the learning, the technology enhances the learning experience, and students can extend their learning outside the four walls of the physical classroom (2017). Training teachers in how to choose the appropriate tools and how to utilize strategies paired with technology to focus on curricular goals can have a deeper impact on student learning than demonstrating how to set up a single web tool.

Setting a Goal and Planning for Professional Learning

Goals help to facilitate growth in a way that is intentional. When a coach is strategically planning internal professional development for a school, the formal sessions provided to staff should remain focused on that singular identified goal. This goal should be linked to the overall vision that has been established for teaching and learning, and should be something that pushes toward the realization of that vision (Figure 3.1). What follows is an example of goals written to align with a vision. Keep in mind that the realization of the vision will not happen overnight and the coach is not solely responsible for all the training, planning, and activities that need to happen to realize the vision. The realization of a vision is the responsibility of everyone who works within the organization.

Keeping the Goal in Mind

When choosing which goal to focus on, consider the needs of the teachers. This can be done through surveys and observations. Additionally, professional learning can take place outside of this regularly scheduled structure according to teacher need, but those sessions should be created as those needs become evident.

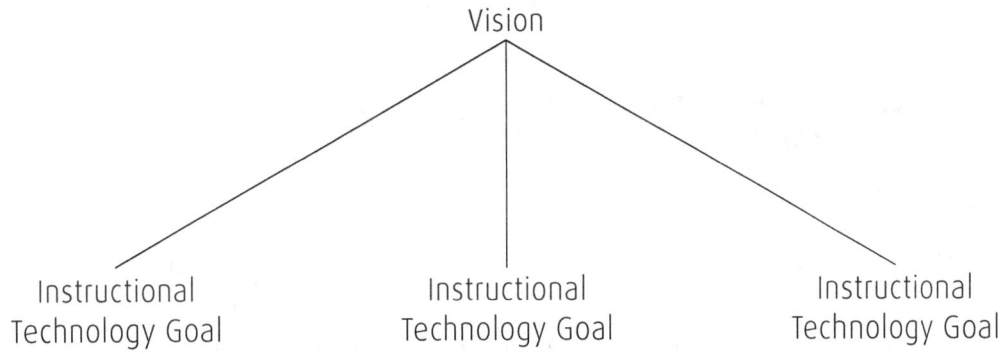

FIGURE 3.1 Break down the vision into achievable and measurable goals.

ISTE STANDARDS FOR COACHES 1A. Create a shared vision and culture for using technology to learn and accelerate transformation through the coaching process.

ISTE STANDARDS FOR COACHES 5A. Design professional learning based on needs assessments and frameworks for working with adults to support their cultural, social-emotional, and learning needs.

One example of this might be the creation of a professional learning experience that centers on the use of collaborative math activities. This session might not be a part of the regularly scheduled plan for professional learning, but the need for the session may be a request from teachers or identified as a need from classroom observations that took place during coaching.

Determining Which Goal to Focus On

While the intention is to remain focused on realizing the vision that has been set for a school or district, the goal for formal professional development can be determined a few different ways. It can be established as a(n):

- District goal
- School goal
- Professional learning community goal
- Individual choice goal

Planning PD for a District or School Goal

District Goal

A district goal may be the best choice for all faculty within a district if there is an identified need that affects all teachers within the schools. Examples might include the adoption of a new instructional framework or the shift from a traditional schedule and delivery of instruction to a newly identified schedule and delivery of instruction (like those required during the COVID-19 pandemic). A district goal may be the hardest of the goals to meet, as it requires a great deal of collaboration and communication between district leadership, school administration, and facilitators of the professional learning to ensure there is alignment across all schools. Focusing on something district-wide can also make it hard for teachers to buy in to the learning. With district level changes happening so often, it is easy for teachers to quickly dismiss professional learning around a district-wide goal as "just another thing that will disappear in a couple years."

School Goal

A school goal can allow faculty and staff of a school community to focus on something that is a unique need of that school. Identifying a school goal can be done in a number of ways: surveys, discussion groups with teachers, needs identified through classroom observations or student data, and other metrics that may be established by the state or national government. For instance, the state of North Carolina requires that every district and charter school evaluate themselves biannually through the use of the North Carolina Digital Learning Progress Rubric (more information about this rubric is available from North Carolina State University's Friday Institute at **ncdli.fi.ncsu.edu/rubric/index.html**). This rubric asks that schools examine their infrastructure, established supports for teachers, and classroom teaching practices. Metrics such as these can help to inform needs that can be addressed through a school's professional learning goal.

District and school-wide goals can provide communities the opportunity to work toward a singular focus. These structures are easier to plan for, but harder to ensure teachers are getting exactly what they feel they need at that moment to help solve problems they may be facing in their classrooms. It is important that teachers are made aware of the data, rationale, and intended outcomes when they are asked to participate in professional learning that is focused on a district or school goal. This is especially true if they were not given a direct voice in the identification of the goal. It is important to be transparent about how the goal was selected and the professional learning created, and how they relate back to the overall vision.

Once a goal is established, it needs to be broken down into bite-size elements that can be explored during regular PD sessions. Brainstorm topics that will help meet the goal and determine if these sessions need to be presented in a specific order. The professional learning planning document (accessible by scanning the QR code) can be used to prepare and present the regularly scheduled professional learning that will be presented to faculty.

The schedule in Table 3.1 demonstrates a plan for a school with a singular focus. This could be completed for the whole staff, or this could be completed for each PLC, where adjustments are made to ensure the PLC's needs are being met.

PROFESSIONAL LEARNING PLANNING DOCUMENT

TABLE 3.1 Plan for School Goal with Singular Focus

GOAL: Generate, analyze, and utilize data to create informed differentiated learning goals for students
SESSIONS MEET: Monthly during PLCs   SESSION LENGTH: 50 minutes

DATE	SESSION TITLE	SESSION DESCRIPTION	SESSION MATERIALS	PREWORK
AUG.	Introduction and Self-Assessment	This session will be used to introduce the goal for the year and provide an opportunity for discussing participants' current usage of data and learning interests on the topic.	Introduction to program materials	Read over the program plan for this year's PD sessions. Bring any questions you may have.

continued

DATE	SESSION TITLE	SESSION DESCRIPTION	SESSION MATERIALS	PREWORK
SEPT.	Integration of Digital Assessments	This session will introduce participants to different ways to assess students using digital applications through a "choose your own adventure" slides activity.	Interactive slides	Complete a reflection chart.
OCT.	Analyzing Assessment Data to Adjust Classroom Lessons	This session looks at assessing different types of data. Participants will explore methods of assessing data according to the type of data they brought with them.	Hyper slides organized by data types	Bring data that you have digitally gathered on students.
NOV.	Generating and Sharing Data as a Team	This session looks at how teams can create common assessments, collaboratively analyze data, and provide support within the team to adjust upcoming lessons to improve learning.	Activity slides Collaborative team document	With your PLC members, choose a standard to focus on that you are going to be teaching in the near future.
DEC.	Student Self-Assessment and Self-Monitoring	This session digs into how students can use self-assessment and monitoring techniques to reflect on their learning, helping them to set their own learning goals.	Learning choice board Student self-monitoring example documentation	Explore resources from the choice board and use the School Reform Initiative's Four A's Text Protocol to reflect on your reading.
JAN.	Creating Individual Learner Profiles	This session allows participants to explore individual learner profiles and how they can be used to identify strengths and needs of students while supporting the creation of lessons that are student-centered.	Self-paced sessions slides Learner profile documentation	Brainstorm a list of ways to collect information about your students. Be ready to share.
FEB.	Reflecting on Instructional Practices	This session allows the participant to reflect on current instructional practices and dig deeper into methods that can be used to complement or enhance their classroom environment.	Reflection protocol	Choose your three best lessons and, in an elevator pitch, be ready to describe them and what makes them successful.

DATE	SESSION TITLE	SESSION DESCRIPTION	SESSION MATERIALS	PREWORK
MAR.	Putting it All Together	This session provides teachers an opportunity to share out their successes with other teachers as they get feedback on documentation that can use for their end of the year evaluation	Face-to-face session	Document of Successes shared with teachers prior to the session.
APR.	Personalizing Instruction	This session offers an opportunity to explore the idea of personalized learning and set participants up to begin planning to implement personalized learning strategies in their classrooms next school year.	Methods of personalization "Choose your own adventure" slides	Read the article "Personalization vs. Differentiation vs. Individualization" by Barbara Bray and Kathleen McClaskey
MAY	"Now What?" Reflection and Next Steps	This session asks participants to reflect on the ways they have changed their utilization of data and asks them to think about what steps they may take to continue to improve data usage in the classroom.	Share out activity document	Complete a reflection document.

Even with the decision to create professional learning that is focused on a district-wide or school-wide goal, there is still a way to implement choice into how that goal is met by providing flexibility that allows participants to engage with the learning sessions when they feel these sessions will most benefit them. For coaches looking to have participants decide when they would like to work through their various professional learning sessions, consider using a session request form like the example provided in Table 3.2. Participants may find that certain sessions fit better with certain curricular topics they will be covering with students at various points in the school year. It is okay to mandate one or two sessions if needed for introduction or conclusion purposes.

PROFESSIONAL LEARNING SESSION REQUEST FORM

TABLE 3.2 Professional Learning Session Request Form

GOAL: Provide teachers with digital teaching and learning strategies that meet their needs. Each month, PLCs will choose one of the professional learning sessions that is most relevant to them.

SESSIONS MEET: Monthly during PLCs   **SESSION LENGTH:** 50 minutes

SESSIONS	SESSION DESCRIPTIONS	DATE REQUESTED
Introduction and Self-Assessment	This session will be used to introduce the goal for the year and provide an opportunity for discussing participants' current usage of data and learning interests on the topic.	Required in August
Integration of Digital Assessments	This session will introduce participants to different ways to assess students using digital applications through a "choose your own adventure" slides activity.	
Analyzing Assessment Data to Adjust Classroom Lessons	This session looks at assessing different types of data. Participants will explore methods of assessing data according to the type of data they brought with them.	
Generating and Sharing Data as a Team	This session looks at how teams can create common assessments, collaboratively analyze data, and provide support within the team to adjust upcoming lessons to improve learning.	
Student Self-Assessment and Self-Monitoring	This session digs into how students can use self-assessment and monitoring techniques to reflect on their learning, helping them to set their own learning goals.	
Creating Individual Learner Profiles	This session allows participants to explore individual learner profiles and how they can be used to identify strengths and needs of students while supporting the creation of lessons that are student-centered.	
Reflecting on Instructional Practices	This session allows the participant to reflect on current instructional practices and dig deeper into methods that can be used to complement or enhance their classroom environment.	
Putting it All Together	This session provides teachers an opportunity to share out their successes with other teachers as they get feedback on documentation that can use for their end of the year evaluation	
Personalizing Instruction	This session offers an opportunity to explore the idea of personalized learning and set participants up to begin planning to implement personalized learning strategies in their classrooms next school year.	
"Now What?" Reflection and Next Steps	This session asks participants to reflect on the ways they have changed their utilization of data and asks them to think about what steps they may take to continue to improve data usage in the classroom.	Required in May

Planning PD for a PLC or Individual Goal

Professional Learning Community Goal

Schools that provide PLC or team time may find that these groups have unique needs from their counterparts found throughout the school. Establishing a goal for professional learning communities allows these groups to really focus on a self-identified need and creates more buy-in as the choice and urgency of exploring the identified topics is directly related to their common curricular needs. Setting goals and establishing formal professional learning at the PLC level can seem daunting, but the educational technology coach's role in this type of structure may not be the same as it is with a district or school goal. While the edtech coach could be creating and facilitating these sessions, some PLCs may find that there is an outside course or program that provides them with professional learning opportunities they would like to take advantage of. This could be something like working to be ISTE-certified or participating in a course provided by a local college of education. Whether the coach is providing the PD or is offering self-paced PD options, an outside source is providing these sessions, or a combination of the two is happening, the edtech coach needs to understand the goals set by the PLC through this learning in order to still offer personalized support that aligns to the goals set by these teachers.

While this is a great option to ensure PLCs are getting their needs met, it is important to remember that the goal is not to set these groups of teachers on a device and leave them to figure out this professional learning alone. A schedule and focus must be maintained while ensuring the other elements of effective professional learning, such as active learning and time for reflection, are still being met. A couple of examples for facilitating this can be found in Table 3.3.

PROFESSIONAL LEARNING SCHEDULE

TABLE 3.3 Planning Professional Learning for PLC Goal

GOAL: Generate, analyze, and utilize data to create informed differentiated learning goals for students
SESSIONS MEET: Monthly during PLCs   **SESSION LENGTH:** 50 minutes

DATE	SESSION TITLE	SESSION DESCRIPTION
AUG.	Introduction and Self-Assessment	This session will be used to introduce the goal for the year and provide an opportunity for discussing participants' current usage of data and learning interests on the topic.
SEPT.	Integration of Digital Assessments	This session will introduce participants to different ways to assess students using digital applications through a "choose your own adventure" slides activity.
OCT.	Analyzing Assessment Data to Adjust Classroom Lessons	This session looks at assessing different types of data. Participants will explore methods of assessing data according to the type of data they brought with them.
NOV.	Generating and Sharing Data as a Team	This session looks at how teams can create common assessments, collaboratively analyze data, and provide support within the team to adjust upcoming lessons to improve learning.
DEC.	Student Self-Assessment and Self-Monitoring	This session digs into how students can use self-assessment and monitoring techniques to reflect on their learning, helping them to set their own learning goals.
JAN.	Creating Individual Learner Profiles	This session allows participants to explore individual learner profiles and how they can be used to identify strengths and needs of students while supporting the creation of lessons that are student-centered.
FEB.	Reflecting on Instructional Practices	This session allows the participant to reflect on current instructional practices and dig deeper into methods that can be used to complement or enhance their classroom environment.
MAR.	Putting it All Together	This session provides teachers an opportunity to share out their successes with other teachers as they get feedback on documentation they can use for their end of the year evaluation.
APR.	Personalizing Instruction	This session offers an opportunity to explore the idea of personalized learning and set participants up to begin planning to implement personalized learning strategies in their classrooms next school year.
MAY	Now What? Reflection and Next Steps	This session asks participants to reflect on the ways they have changed their utilization of data and asks them to think about what steps they may take to continue to improve data usage in the classroom.

SESSION FORMAT	SESSION MATERIALS	PREWORK
Session with edtech coach and school administration	Introduction to program materials	Read over the program plan for this year's PD sessions. Bring any questions you may have.
Online session with collaborative activity completed during PLC time	Interactive slides	Complete a reflection chart.
Session with (expert teacher name here)	Hyper slides organized by data types	Bring data that you have digitally gathered on students.
Session with the principal	Activity slides Collaborative team document	With your PLC members, choose a standard to focus on that you are going to be teaching in the near future.
Online session with collaborative activity completed during PLC time	Learning choice board Student self-monitoring example documentation	Explore resources from the choice board and use the School Reform Initiative's Four A's Text Protocol to reflect on your reading.
Session with (expert teacher name here)	Self-paced sessions slides Learner profile documentation	Brainstorm a list of ways you collect information about your students. Be ready to share.
Session with edtech coach	Reflection protocol	Choose your three best lessons and, in an elevator pitch, be ready to describe them and what makes them successful.
Face-to-face session	Document of Successes shared with teachers prior to the session	Prepare Document of Successes to share with the group.
Online session with collaborative activity completed during PLC time	Methods of personalization "Choose your own adventure" slides	Read the article "Personalization vs. Differentiation vs. Individualization" by Barbara Bray and Kathleen McClaskey.
Face-to-face session with principal	Share out activity document	Complete a reflection document.

Individual Goal through Choice

Another option is to have teachers choose professional learning goals that are focused on their individualized needs. This can be accomplished a couple of ways. One way is to offer multiple professional learning options through pathways. Participants choose a goal to focus on and follow that chosen pathway throughout the duration of the professional learning, as seen in Table 3.4, with goals listed below.

PROFESSIONAL LEARNING CHOICE BOARD

Goal 1: Engage in leadership opportunities in digital teaching and learning.

Goal 2: Enhance classroom use of digital content and instruction.

Goal 3: Generate, analyze, and utilize data to create informed differentiated learning goals for students.

Goal 4: Understand and embed digital citizenship within the classroom.

TABLE 3.4 Sample Planning Chart for Individual Goal through Choice

	GOAL 1	GOAL 2	GOAL 3	GOAL 4
AUG.	Enroll	Enroll	Enroll	Enroll
SEPT.	Introduction and self-assessment	Introduction and self-assessment	Introduction and self-assessment	Introduction and self-assessment
OCT.	Growth mindset	Educational goal setting	Integration of digital assessments	Digital equity
NOV.	What is a connected educator?	Choosing appropriate digital tools for instruction	Student self-assessment and self-monitoring	Creating a culture of respect
DEC.	Sharing—even when it is difficult	Student empowerment through collaboration and creativity	Creating individual learner profiles	Integrating digital citizenship in your lessons
JAN.	Virtual collaboration	Analyzing authentic problems	Reflecting on instructional practices	Using digital tools to take your classroom global
FEB.	Reflecting: the step that is often skipped	Genius hour	Personalizing instruction	Copyright, intellectual property, and fair use

	GOAL 1	GOAL 2	GOAL 3	GOAL 4
MAR.	Putting it all together: products for evaluation	Putting it all together: products for evaluation	Putting it all together: products for evaluation	Putting it all together: products for evaluation
APR.	Leadership in your school	Flexible learning environments	Generating and sharing data as a team	Professional digital social interaction
MAY	Share final products and reflections	Share final products and reflections	Share final products and reflections	Share final products and reflections

Another way to offer teachers a choice is to provide the time for the teachers to work on a program that is provided outside of their school system. This could include participating in the ISTE Certification course, Google Certification, or course from another outside entity that provides professional learning focused on skills the teacher is interested in learning. When having a teacher go outside of the school for their chosen professional learning, the educational technology coach can still provide the same support outside of the PD that is offered to teachers who are utilizing internal professional learning. To do this, the educational technology coach should be aware of the goals for the professional learning program chosen by the teacher and should work to have resources readily available to provide coaching and personalized support that focus on those goals.

Necessary Qualities Within Professional Learning Sessions

When the educational technology coach provides professional learning for staff, there are some simple ways to ensure participants are getting the most out of these sessions by offering sessions that:

- utilize small groups,
- embed choice,
- are considerate of time,
- engage participants in active learning, and
- rely on feedback for appropriate adjustments.

PROFESSIONAL LEARNING SESSION PLANNING DOCUMENT

TABLE 3.5 Example of Professional Learning Session Planning Sheet

OVERALL PROFESSIONAL LEARNING GOAL:	
Session Title:	Date:
Session Objectives:	Session Length:
Materials:	Session Pre-work:
Session Activities:	Session Attributes: ☐ Active Learning ☐ Choice
Feedback Survey:	

Utilizing Small Groups

Large faculty meetings are not the best forum for professional learning. Small, focused groups can make the sessions that are planned more meaningful to participants. Consider providing professional learning sessions to groups made of teachers who teach the same grade level or who teach the same subject matter (traditional groupings for school-based professional learning communities). While PLCs are a popular method that allow for some fantastic and curriculum-focused collaboration, remember that putting teachers into groups outside of their traditional PLCs can also provide collaboration that can prove to be a catalyst for pedagogical change. For example, art teachers often provide hands-on learning activities for their students. A traditional content area teacher may be able to collaborate with an art teacher to better understand how to facilitate exploratory and project-focused learning activities within science or math classes. There can be great value in mixed groupings for teachers.

If your priority is to offer teacher choice, then teachers may also group themselves. Provide options that allow them to choose what they learn about from a menu or choice board. This approach may be especially relevant if one of your school goals is to have teachers provide students with more choice within their classrooms. If teachers can feel what it is to have such options as learners themselves, they may be more willing to allow students more choice in their learning.

Look back at the vision and goals that have been established as your focus. Knowing the goals and the teachers who are in the school should help to establish what groupings are going to benefit your school the most. It is okay to create groups, and it is okay to make changes to grouping choices as the need arises. Just like teachers need to be flexible with their student groupings, professional learning needs to have flexibility to make sure participants are not being pushed too fast or being forced to waste time by working through material that does not apply to them.

Embedding Choice

Choice can be provided by allowing teachers to choose what they learn and how they demonstrate that learning. Professional learning sessions focused on pedagogical strategies instead of individual tools can allow for choice in the same ways teachers can offer choice to students. Session facilitators can offer choice in:

- where and when participants engage with resources,
- which resources participants engage with, and
- what tools participants use to implement the skill.

Teachers need to know that the sessions they are attending are useful to their daily work and help them to solve the problems or concerns they face daily in the classroom. When planning professional development, think about the environment your teachers are working in each day and look at the standards they are asked to meet and the types of lessons they are creating. Then ask yourself, "Where could our teachers embed more choice?" Start there. Model for teachers the choices they can give their students, then be transparent about how you set up the learning session to provide these choices. Make it clear that the educational technology coach is there to help support teachers who are ready to utilize these techniques in their own classes. Modeling choice in this way can open the door for a collaborative planning and teaching experience. By implementing it into the professional learning session itself, the teachers better understand how having such options can empower the learner.

Choice in when to engage in resources

One strategy for embedding choice is to have teachers choose where they want to do their learning. While many may find that having time during professional learning sessions to engage with resources such as videos, readings, or audio clips helps them to allocate time devoted specifically to professional learning, consider sending these resources a week or so in advance of the session. This gives participants the option to take more time with the resources. Consider keeping some of that time planned in the session to engage with the resources and let participants know that there is time to do this or that they can come later for the activity portion of the session (McBride & Dirkin, 2020). For example, an hour-long session is scheduled to begin after school at 4:00. Participants have the option to show up at 4:00 to read, watch, or listen to the resources that were sent. Alternately, if they choose to engage with these materials on their own time, they can come in at 4:20 to participate in the collaborative activities planned for the remainder of the session.

Choice in which resources to engage with

When choosing resources that inspire thought around different pedagogical practices or ideals, there are often a great many journal articles, blog posts, podcasts, and videos to choose from. Provide participants a choice by curating materials that cover the same topic, writing a very short summary of the resource, and asking them to engage in only a certain number of these resources. Make sure to provide variety in the types that are offered and consider looking for some that are subject- and grade-specific so teachers can see variations that are directly applicable to what they teach. This allows for even richer discussion during collaborative activities, and participants may explore more than the requested number of resources.

Choice in tools participants use to implement the skill

Just because the professional learning offered by the educational technology coach should be focused on pedagogical practices does not mean that teachers should not be provided guidance in which tools are out there to help them to better implement the practice they are learning. Consider offering a small number of suggested tools to help teachers implement their learning with students and offering to provide additional guidance for how to set up and use that tool with their students as a curricular support. It may also be beneficial to carve out a small amount of time within the session for participants to explore these tool suggestions and play around with them. For example, a session that focuses on how to set up blended learning that utilizes student data to inform instruction could end with a few suggestions of formative assessment tools that allow the instructor to easily see what each student is struggling to understand. The teacher can explore this tool alone or request a follow-up with the coach to help set up and use the tool that will work best for the teacher.

Timing Is Everything

Time is precious. In fact, it is the most precious commodity we have to offer. Consider the timing of professional learning and make sure that the time teachers are asked to participate in these sessions is not wasted. This is why the structure of how the educational technology coach plans to provide professional learning sessions is so important. Additionally, the coach's time is equally as valuable. So for some—especially those in larger schools—jumping from one PLC or small group to the next is not sustainable if the coach wishes to provide in-depth coaching, offer time to provide content-focused support, and maintain focus on other leadership responsibilities. While we will visit more scheduling strategies for the educational technology coach in chapter 7, let's look at one possible solution for utilizing time wisely when it comes to providing these regular professional learning sessions.

Because coaches should be facilitators of the learning and not stand-and-deliver professional developers, they could have multiple professional learning sessions happening simultaneously through the use of blended learning strategies. Imagine multiple groups of teachers coming into a session and sitting in smaller learning groups. They are made aware of where to begin because it has been posted in their learning management system. The coach has provided the session activities and resources, and the instructions given through their LMS allows teachers to explore and collaborate together on their learning. The coach works with groups as needed, but the learning is primarily driven by the learners. Outside of just saving time, a scenario like this exposes teachers to different resources, digital platforms, and strategies that they can turn around and use with their students as they differentiate learning in their classrooms to meet the needs of their students.

Use of Active Learning Strategies

The professional learning opportunities offered by the educational technology coach need to incorporate active learning strategies that allow participants to collaborate with one another and engage with the content. This can get loud, and that is great!

MODELING WITH TEACHERS

Brad Shreffler, Instructional Technology Coach

In my eight or so years as an instructional technology coach, I have had the great pleasure to build up two successful 1:1 initiatives at the largest high school in the country and then the largest middle school in the country. While any coach will tell you that we wear many hats, when I am asked by those starting as coaches what the key to success of my implementations has been, I say *modeling*. It is true that relationship-building, communication, flexibility, lesson co-planning, etc. are all critical tools in the repertoire of a coach, but when it comes to how to get teachers to use technology tools in their classrooms to increase student learning, it is *modeling* that matters.

Far too often we build sessions that begin with explaining what a tool does and then how to use it, but that is the wrong order of events. When I am set to instruct teachers in a new instructional technology tool, I always start with putting the teachers into the student perspective of the tool. In fact, I often say that if you can't use the tool to teach the tool, it isn't going to be successful. So when starting a session on how to use Nearpod, the first thing teachers will do is join a session as a student. If I'm explaining a new learning management system, the training is built into that system.

There are two primary benefits to this method. The first is that the teacher will understand what students will go through when using the new tool for the first time. In my first year as an instructional technology coach, I would get tons of emails and phone calls every period asking what a student needed to do to join a session, submit an assignment, or create a copy of something. I had not started with modeling then; I had started with the teacher perspective, and so there were gaps in my teachers' knowledge.

The second benefit—and this is the one that really matters—is that this allows teachers to see the "why" for a specific tool before having to figure out the "how." I call myself an instructional technology coach because instruction is first. When teachers understand what the tool can do for students, then they can determine the best places and times to use that tool as leverage for student learning. If a teacher sees that Flipgrid allows the student to create quick and easy video responses to a prompt, then they start to develop ideas for how to use it in their content and in their classroom. *Their* creative ideas, not mine. *Their* innovative uses, not mine. *Their* collective brilliance, not mine.

There is no more powerful a tool than the minds of our teachers, and when we engage that first, the tool becomes infinitely more useful.

Participants engaged in active learning should be given tasks that allow them to play with the ideas that they are being asked to learn (University of Minnesota, 2020). This could mean providing an activity that asks teachers to pull apart ideas presented to them and brainstorm with their colleges through the use of graphic organizers. It could mean that they participate in a jigsaw activity that has them interacting in different capacities within their own small group or moving around the room to engage with multiple groups. It could also mean that they take their learning and actively practice the skills by planning a lesson with their group mates. When creating professional development, it is okay to do a web search for "active learning strategies." There are some fantastic resources with activities that coaches can use to ensure their sessions are engaging and meaningful. The best part is, the more active learning strategies the coach utilizes in these sessions, the more examples of activities the teachers whom the coach works with will have been exposed to.

ISTE STANDARDS FOR COACHES 5B. Build the capacity of educators, leaders, and instructional teams to put the ISTE Standards into practice by facilitating active learning and providing meaningful feedback.

Feedback and Adjusting Professional Learning Plans

It is okay to adjust professional learning plans as problems arise. If the coach notices that there is a need to provide more time or more activities around a particular topic, then it becomes necessary to adjust the planned schedule. It is also okay to have activities fail during professional learning sessions. Active learning and exploratory learning can get messy. Do not hesitate to try new methods. When one fails, be open with staff about that failure and ask participants to help the facilitator of the learning to figure out what went wrong so they can use that information if they decide to try the activity with their own students.

ISTE STANDARDS FOR COACHES 5C. Evaluate impact of professional learning and continually make improvements in order to meet schoolwide vision for using technology for high-impact teaching and learning.

Regardless of whether the session came out exactly as planned or was a complete failure, it is important to request feedback from participants. This can be done quickly through the use of a number of survey- or form-builders. The feedback should be looked at and used to help adjust upcoming sessions. The utilization for feedback can help ensure participants are feeling that the time they spend in professional learning is valuable and meeting their needs for growth. There are many options when creating this form, but consider working with a survey instrument that can utilize a portion of a whole evaluation model for your professional learning setup. One such model that can be utilized is the Professional Development Evaluation Framework for the Ohio ABLE system, developed by the Center on Education and Training for Employment at Ohio State University (2010). The ABLE evaluation provides questions for participants to provide feedback after each session, as well as questions to help assess the program overall.

PROFESSIONAL DEVELOPMENT EVALUATION FRAMEWORK FOR THE OHIO ABLE SYSTEM

Session feedback is not the only way for coaches to evaluate the impact of their professional learning sessions. Observations of teachers and their utilization of the strategies presented in professional learning can also be a key indicator of a successful or unsuccessful session. Keep an eye out for implementations and opportunities to support those implementations through personalized teacher supports. Teachers may not implement strategies immediately because they need these ideas to be modeled, co-planned, and co-taught to better understand how what they were presented in the professional learning can be used within the context of their own classrooms.

 **ISTE STANDARDS FOR COACHES 2C.** Establish shared goals with educators, reflect on successes and continually improve coaching and teaching practice.

With a structured professional learning plan, the coach already has a place to facilitate learning for teachers. This element of the educational technology coach's role can be the jumping-off point for many of the collaborations that can happen as the coach digs deeper into supporting teachers and their individual needs through personalized support and coaching.

Professional Development Checklist

- [ ] A goal based on our vision has been established for this year's professional learning plan. The goal for professional learning will be:
    - [ ] District-based
    - [ ] School-based
    - [ ] PLC-based
    - [ ] Individual choice
- [ ] Sessions have been scheduled regularly throughout the year:
    - [ ] How often will this formal professional development take place? _____
    - [ ] Each session will last approximately _____ minutes/hours (circle one).
    - [ ] Where will these sessions be held? _____
- [ ] Participants have access to the session list and understand the learning goal.

Individual Planning by Session

- [ ] Each planned session is focused on pedagogical practices aligned with the goal.
- [ ] Pre-work was:
    - [ ] Not necessary
    - [ ] Assigned in advance so participants can effectively engage in the session
- [ ] There is no wasted time during the session.
- [ ] Active learning strategies that can be taken back to the classroom have been used within the session:
    - [ ] Participants can access the source material so they can recreate the activity.
- [ ] Choice has been embedded in (choose at least one):
    - [ ] What was learned
    - [ ] How the participant learned
    - [ ] How learning was demonstrated
    - [ ] Pace or order of learning
- [ ] A feedback survey is provided at the end of the session.

4

PROVIDING PERSONALIZED SUPPORT TO TEACHERS

The most effective educational technology coaches are not simply great professional developers. While that is a good starting point, teachers need more. They need a *partner*: Someone they can work with to help them find a new strategy or resource. Someone who can be there to bounce teaching ideas back and forth with them. They need a person who is able to be in the room with them as they implement a new strategy or technology. They need someone who will not be judgmental but will support them and help them find a silver lining when they have tried something and it failed.

The basis of being able to offer teachers this kind of support is embedded in the relationship the coach has with the teachers with whom the coach works. The coach cannot be seen as an evaluator or as another administrator. If the teacher is going to be willing to ask for the support the coach can offer, then the teacher needs to know that the edtech coach can be trusted.

The teacher also needs to know that while reflecting on teaching practices, trying—and possibly failing—at new implementations, and talking through classroom struggles and strategies with the coach, these conversations are not being taken back to anyone, especially individuals who are evaluating the teacher. The point of the educational technology coach is to relieve some of the stresses and anxieties that can come with trying new teaching strategies and technologies.

The tricky part is, every teacher is different. Every teacher has a different need and a different preference about how they want to be supported. I have worked with teachers who came to me only for resources. Once they had a solution to the classroom problem they wanted to solve, they would take that solution and run with it. Others wanted more 1:1 support. I would spend time helping them plan, set up the lesson, and model the instructional practice, then move out of the way once they felt comfortable with taking off on their own. Then there were those who were somewhere in between, and some of these preferences can even change according to the topic or focus of the teacher at the time.

The support offered by the edtech coach needs to be personalized to the teacher, but the supports themselves generally fall within these focus areas:

- research
- co-planning
- co-teaching
- modeling
- data analysis and usage

Research

I had a conversation with an educational technology coach in which we talked about how we found resources for our teachers. One thing that stood out was a comment made about how she felt she could not spend time during school researching because the administration did not understand that when she was at her computer searching and reading, she was looking for resources for her teachers.

Time and space to research is an important component of the educational technology coach's role. The edtech coach is especially equipped to provide better and more personalized support to teachers when they take the time and space to make research a regular facet of their day-to-day job where they can "keep current with emerging technology and innovations in pedagogy and the learning sciences" (ISTE Standard for Coaches 2b). The edtech coach will often be asked questions or have requests made to provide input on a specific resource or strategy, or to help provide a technology-related solution to a particular problem. For the times when coaches are faced with instances they are not familiar with or questions to which they do not have a readily available answer, a response of "Let me see what I can find for you" can be the most powerful. Remember, being an edtech coach is *not* about having all the answers. Being an edtech coach is about knowing how to look for solutions and how to process that research so teachers have an ally they can turn to for support in collaboratively solving problems.

ISTE STANDARDS FOR COACHES 2B. Actively participate in professional learning networks to enhance coaching practice and keep current with emerging technology and innovations in pedagogy and the learning sciences.

The role of research for the edtech coach is not solely for solving known problems with teachers. Keeping up-to-date on the latest trends and practices also provides opportunities for coaches to offer strategies that can enhance the learning experience in ways that have not been imagined within the school before. So it is okay for a coach to spend some dedicated time each week to just research pedagogy and emerging technology. Blocking out some time devoted specifically to this is essential to the creation of effective professional development, providing new solutions during co-planning, and offering constructive feedback and support during coaching cycles. It is important to note that while scientific research journals and academic writings are an essential resource, more anecdotal and experiential resources are also effective and often provide a practical application that is easier to relate back to the classroom environment. A collaborative list of resources and research, including Twitter hashtags and blogs, can be found at **edtechcoachingprimer.com**.

Co-Planning

Co-planning was always my favorite part of being an educational technology coach. I still enjoy planning instruction with teachers and the edtech coaches I currently work with. Co-planning gives those involved the opportunity to collaborate on the creation of a lesson or unit. That collaboration allows for learning experiences to be reimagined and made more impactful, while giving the coach the ability to provide support as a learning designer. Whether the co-planning session leads to a modeling or co-teaching experience, or it is a standalone activity, the coach is there to support the teacher—or even a small group of teachers—with:

- developing active learning experiences for students,
- promoting student agency within the lesson,
- implementing the appropriate digital tool to assess learning and provide timely feedback,
- accommodating learner variability, and
- incorporating digital citizenship into curricula for authentic experiences.

ISTE STANDARDS FOR COACHES 4A. Collaborate with educators to develop authentic, active learning experiences that foster student agency, deepen content mastery and allow students to demonstrate their competency.

ISTE STANDARDS FOR COACHES 4B. Help educators use digital tools to create effective assessments that provide timely feedback and support personalized learning.

The co-planning meetings themselves need to be more than a brainstorming session. There needs to be a completed product at the conclusion of the collaboration, whether that takes one or multiple sessions. Coming prepared and maintaining focus on the task at hand is important, as time is a precious commodity during the school day. Utilizing a structure for these collaborations can ensure the time spent co-planning is productive and effective.

Before the Co-Planning Meeting

Once a teacher or teachers has scheduled a co-planning meeting, it is important to make sure the goals of the session are understood and the coach has enough awareness of the lesson or unit's focus to be able to pull some preliminary research, notes, or technology resources. Sending the teacher(s) a quick questionnaire in an email or asking a few questions informally

BEFORE CO-PLANNING SESSION QUESTIONS

prior to the meeting can help build that necessary understanding of what to expect when heading into the co-planning session. Following are four questions that can provide enough background for preparations.

1. What standards will this lesson/unit focus on?

2. Is this a lesson/unit we will build from scratch, or is this an existing lesson we are looking to improve? (If it is a lesson that is being improved, request access to past lesson plans.)

3. Is there any specific element of this lesson you want to focus on?

    ☐ Assessment of the standards

    ☐ Active learning

    ☐ Differentiation

    ☐ Incorporating digital citizenship

    ☐ Development of a learning environment

    ☐ Other _____

4. Are there any specific web resources, applications, or technologies that you were wanting to try within this lesson/unit?

Be mindful that these questions are flexible, as are the suggested checklist items for number 3. If there is a specific school or professional learning goal that needs to be addressed here, adding a question or suggested list item is appropriate. Also consider that adding too many questions can be more work than is necessary on the teacher(s). The goal is always to make these personalized supports as useful to the teachers as possible without adding unnecessary burdens or requirements to their plates. The simple responses elicited by these questions should not take more than a couple minutes to construct and will save time during the co-planning session, making the collaboration more productive.

During the Co-Planning Meeting

There is a tricky balance to maintain during any 1:1 or small group planning session (for simplicity, the rest of this section is written as if co-planning were taking place with a single teacher, even though it is also common practice to do this with multiple teachers who may be working on a similar lesson together). There needs to be time and space to brainstorm and play with ideas, but at some point decisions need to be made, plans need to be drafted, and a final product needs to be established so preparations can be made to implement the plans. Structuring the steps of the session can be helpful to keep the planning on track and productive. Table 4.1 is a suggested protocol for such a planning session. The example is of a ninety-minute session (ten minutes left out to account for expected overage). The times listed are rough estimates and can be adjusted to reflect needs. Some collaborations—especially collaborations that are planning entire units—can take longer and require stretching this protocol out to multiple meetings.

CO-PLANNING AGENDA

TABLE 4.1 Sample Agenda for Co-Planning Session

TIME ESTIMATE	FOCUS	NOTES
10 minutes	Teacher talks it out	
10 minutes	Successes and struggle points: • students in the class • past implementations of the lesson/unit	
5 minutes	What I heard	
5 minutes	Define goals	
10 minutes	What-ifs	
15 minutes	Draft	
15 minutes	Walk through and adjust	
10 minutes	Plan next steps	

Teacher Talks It Out

A teacher who is looking to co-plan has no doubt thought about the lesson or unit in some way prior to the meeting. It is important to let teachers talk through all of the thoughts they have had about the lesson. This allows teachers to lead the discussion and provides the coach with a better understanding of what teachers are looking for as far as outcomes for the collaboration.

Success and Struggle Points

When planning with a teacher—especially if it is a new partnership—it is good to get a sense of any successes the teacher has had with the students for whom the lesson is being designed. It is equally necessary to understand any struggles the teacher has with this class (it could be something as simple as the students having a lack of focus because it is the last class of the day). Information like this could lead to discussions of how to bring in more high-energy active learning strategies that engage students in the content through physical movement. If the lesson or unit is something that the teacher has used before, having the same reflective conversation about the successful elements and those that the teacher felt were a struggle can provide the coach information about resources that already exist and provide some jumping-off points as the lesson is redesigned.

What I Heard

There is nothing more frustrating than participating in a meeting where one person has completely misunderstood the thoughts and intentions of the other. Now that the teacher has shared the ideas or vision about the lesson/unit and reflected on the successes and struggles, the coach can prevent misunderstandings by making an "I heard" statement. This approach allows coaches to lay out what they heard a teacher say and gives teachers an opportunity to clear up any misunderstandings about what they are looking to accomplish through the co-planning experience.

Define Goals

At this point in the conversation, defining or just simply restating the goal or goals for the lesson or unit being planned can bring back the focus needed to begin moving forward. Write the goals down and make it easily viewable while designing the plan so it can remain the focus throughout the rest of the co-planning session.

What-Ifs

Here is a chance to take all that information—the teacher's shared reflection and experiences, plus the coach's understanding and experience—and really look at some options for creating a stellar lesson or unit. Just start with the words "What if . . . ?" and brainstorm from there. This could be done as a timed activity or just used as a conversation starter. Write everything down, no matter how big or impossible it may seem, as long as it associates with the goal.

Draft

With everything out on the table and all of the brainstormed ideas out for everyone to see and process, it is time to draft the plan. What will assessment look like? How will you get students ready to show understanding? What activity will be first? Second? How will you ensure understanding throughout? All of these questions go into planning any lesson, and co-planning is no different.

Walk Through and Adjust

As the coach and the teacher complete the draft of the lesson/unit, walk through the steps of the lesson delivery. If this is a precursor to a co-teaching experience, this is a good time to assign roles and define who will be doing what, when, and with which students. Make adjustments to the lesson and touch up materials or resources that will be used by the teacher and the students during the lesson.

Plan Next Steps

Now that the lesson or unit is planned, what preparations need to be made? If this is a co-teaching scenario, who will take responsibility for that? This is also a good time to schedule a reflection session that takes place after the implementation of the lesson or unit.

After the Co-Planning Meeting

While co-planning can be something that happens on its own, there are often missed opportunities when the co-planning experience is not followed up with co-teaching, modeling, observation, reflection, or a combination of these. The continued support that comes with co-teaching and modeling can provide teachers with a partner in the classroom, while observation and/or reflection can provide more in-depth knowledge about what strategies are effective, how to improve them, and what other support needs the teacher may have.

Modeling

Seeing or experiencing something as it happens is a powerful learning strategy. When teachers are asked to implement strategies they are not familiar with, it can be frustrating because they may not have had the chance to see or experience these strategies firsthand. This is why modeling is such an important element of the educational technology coach's role. Modeling can happen in a few different places:

- professional learning sessions
- within the classroom alongside students
- lesson design
- their own professional learning
- digital citizenship

ISTE STANDARDS FOR COACHES 4D. Model the use of instructional design principles with educators to create effective digital learning environments.

Professional learning sessions are a perfect place to model good instructional practices. Teachers need the opportunity to see different teaching and learning strategies in action. By placing teachers in the position of the learners and asking them to engage in their learning differently, teachers are able to better understand how students would feel in that learning structure.

Within the Classroom Alongside Students

Modeling in the classroom is different from co-teaching. While co-teaching requires the teacher and coach to plan and implement the lesson together, modeling within a classroom indicates that the educational technology coach is taking on the responsibility of teaching the lesson or unit for a specific class or a defined amount of time. This is most effective when the teacher has co-planned the lesson and understands what the goals of the lesson are. The lesson itself is implemented by the coach, but the teacher is in the room to observe.

This tactic is especially effective if the coach is working with the teacher on understanding how a practice can be implemented. Modeling can allow the teacher a way to see the strategy in action. When this is done in professional learning (as previously described in this chapter), the teacher may still question whether the strategy is truly usable with students. The coach can model the strategy with students so the teacher can see and grasp how utilization of that strategy can be accomplished. Once the teacher has observed the strategy, the coach can have the teacher implement the strategy either in a co-teaching scenario or solo. The coach can provide support by being present and observing, which can lead right into a formal coaching cycle.

ISTE STANDARDS FOR COACHES 3D. Personalize support for educators by planning and modeling the effective use of technology to improve student learning.

The ISTE Standards for Students and the ISTE Standards for Educators have been adopted by a number of states around the country. Modeling the implementation of these standards can happen both in professional learning and when co-planning lessons with teachers. When creating professional learning sessions, consider sharing the professional lesson planning document with teachers. Post the ISTE Standards for Educators and the ISTE Standards for Students that the methods you are utilizing during the training would meet if you were implementing those methods within a student lesson. While co-planning lessons alongside teachers, help them to align their plans with the ISTE Standards for Students. These actions, while they may seem small, will help to keep the technology alignment standards provided by ISTE in front of teachers and help them to understand how you are supporting teachers with their standards alignment. These actions will also demonstrate what methodologies can be used to meet some of the standards they are asked to meet with their students.

In the Edtech Coach's Professional Learning

Modeling by the educational technology coach continues beyond teaching and the creation of lesson plans. Edtech coaches should model the attitude of lifelong learners through continuous personal goal setting, participation in professional learning networks, and taking on learning challenges to help them grow in their coaching practices. If the coach is responsible for helping to support the growth of the teachers, there should be intentionality in making sure the *coach* is focused on growing, as well. There are more detailed information and resources for this in chapter 8.

Digital Citizenship

Digital citizenship is a life necessity. Thinking critically about the media that we and our students consume, the information we give away, and the exchanges we have with others online is not something that should be taught in a vacuum. These lessons and conversations should be taking place daily and in the context of every interaction that is had in the digital environment. This can be modeled by the educational technology coach through each lesson created or cocreated, each coaching conversation, and each resource conversation with teachers.

ISTE STANDARDS FOR COACHES 7B. Partner with educators, leaders, students and families to foster a culture of respectful online interactions and a healthy balance in their use of technology.

ISTE STANDARDS FOR COACHES 7D. Empower educators, leaders, and students to make informed decisions to protect their personal data and curate the digital profile they intend to reflect.

In lesson design and delivery, the coach can remind learners of online norms that are relevant to the environment they are working in. For example, "Remember, when you are posting comments to your classmates' work, you need to keep in mind how you word your responses. The tone of your writing is important. We are a team, and we want to support each other in our learning journey." During coaching conversations, the edtech coach can relate opportunities for these exchanges to take place during the lessons that were observed. And when sharing resources with teachers, take a moment to explain how the resource protects student data privacy and how the teacher can integrate digital citizenship activities and conversations as students begin using the resource.

Co-Teaching

Co-teaching is not something that has to happen after a lesson is co-planned, but co-planning should happen *before* a co-teaching experience. Co-teaching is a partnership between the coach and the teacher, where each of these individuals takes responsibility for implementing the planned lesson. This is not simply providing "tech support" to students while they try a new technology. In a true co-teaching environment, the educational technology coach will support instruction through the same methods the classroom teacher would implement. For example, a planned lesson may incorporate blended learning through the use of stations. With a co-teacher, this could become even more effective, as one individual could provide students with a small group lesson while the other facilitates student exploration of a topic in another station.

ISTE STANDARDS FOR COACHES 3A. Establish trusting and respectful coaching relationships that encourage educators to explore new instructional strategies.

A co-teaching experience can help to "encourage educators to explore new instructional strategies" (ISTE Standard for Coaches 3a). A teacher who has only used direct instruction methods, individual assignments, or grouped students to complete the same task at the same time may hesitate to try something like a station rotation blended learning model. With the edtech coach acting as a co-teacher in these types of instances, the teacher can feel more confident and able to implement this type of learning experience, allowing for the teacher to begin to utilize these strategies without the coach.

MAKING AN AMAZING LESSON THROUGH COLLABORATION

Connie Wolf, Instructional Technology Facilitator

"What's new out there? We want some spice."

Our seventh-grade science teachers had hit a wall. They had taught body systems before, and each time students turned in the same surface-level Google Slides. So in an effort to increase engagement, they asked their instructional technology facilitator (me) and librarian (Gabriel) how their students could make podcasts, screencasts, and videos of what they would learn.

Gabriel and I met with the seventh-grade science team, and since they already had ideas about what products they wanted students to create, we began by asking about the lessons leading up to the final project. What was the big idea they wanted the projects to capture? What had students struggled with in previous body system units? The answer was surprising: Students weren't engaging deep enough with the material. They weren't grasping that all body systems were interconnected and that diseases affecting one body system would affect others.

Providing more final product options wasn't going to address these issues, so we paused our discussion about podcasts, screencasts, etc. and began brainstorming. To increase the depth of their knowledge base, we decided to give students more time to research individual body systems (using databases recommended by Gabriel and an online simulation recommended by me). Students would complete research in groups, and after everyone had become an expert on one body system, they would teach other groups about that system. In these "jigsaw" groups, students would be able to compare notes and discover the ways their systems connected. To further prompt them to discuss the systems' interdependence, though, we decided that students' motivation for their jigsaw would be an impending disease.

At the time of the unit, Thanos had just dusted half the population in *Avengers: Infinity War*. So, being Marvel fans, we put together a trailer where Thanos threatened to dust the body if students didn't sacrifice one of its systems. To help us develop the structures that students would use to debate, negotiate, and make a plan for defeating this "disease," I recruited a seventh-grade social studies teacher. He was happy to teach students about diplomacy in his class (as well as play Thanos in our trailer!). This allowed the students to think about and connect ideas across curricular barriers. The social studies teacher's contribution meant the science teachers could, as they put it, focus on "[guiding] students to the conclusion that all . . . body systems work together to enable us to function properly."

By the end of the unit, the science team observed that "more . . . students were able to reach the correct conclusion [by completing this project] than when [they, as teachers,] used a previous project." The design changes—made when co-planning with Gabriel, the science teachers, our social studies teacher, and me—had produced deeper student understanding, in addition to a series of creative, interdisciplinary learning experiences we were all proud to have a hand in.

5

Implementing Formal Coaching Cycles

Teachers are familiar with observation and evaluation cycles. A certain number of observations and feedback meetings are prescribed throughout the year, where an administrator (and sometimes a colleague) will come into the room, to observe and evaluate the lesson through the use of a rubric or walk-through document. These events may be scheduled or pop-in, and while administrators may intend for these to be supportive in nature, the fact that there is a measuring stick being used to determine "teacher effectiveness" can become nerve-racking and stressful as teachers feel they are being graded rather than supported. The intention behind these is to get teachers to think about their practice, get feedback from administration, and make a plan to improve. Yet when a measure is involved, sometimes the focus of the improvement is not centered on student or teacher growth; instead it becomes centered around obtaining a higher score on the evaluation rubric.

Data Analysis and Usage

For many, *data* is a four-letter word that does not inspire excitement. In my second year as an educational technology coach, my principal came to me and asked that I lead the school's data team. I took the position, but in all honesty, I wasn't sure what I was expected to do. With her guidance, however, and a fantastic team of teachers, we were able to agree on the utilization of an action research cycle that we would adapt to meet our school's need for a data cycle. From there, we were able to break down the steps for gathering data, analyzing it, and adjusting instruction according to the findings. It was a great learning process for me and gave me a deeper appreciation for the critical role data plays in implementing blended, differentiated, and personalized learning environments. This is why the educational technology coach should be situated to support teachers in their use of data in the classroom.

 **ISTE STANDARDS FOR COACHES 6B.** Support educators to interpret qualitative and quantitative data to inform their decisions and support individual student learning.

Because the educational technology coach is in a position that is non-evaluative, teachers may be more willing to honestly share their classroom data with the coach. This gives the edtech coach the opportunity to work with the teacher to establish data norms that can help influence instructional practices. A great resource for understanding how to coach teachers in the use of data to promote better student outcomes is *The Data Coach's Guide to Improving Learning for All Students* (Love, 2008). This resource provides in-depth discussion not only about coaching teachers through data but also the establishment and utilization of data teams at the school level for overall school improvement. However, the educational technology coach doesn't necessarily have to go to the extent of full-fledged data coaching, which is a job in itself.

 **ISTE STANDARDS FOR COACHES 6A.** Assist educators and leaders in securely collecting and analyzing student data.

Instead, the edtech coach can focus on instructional strategies that promote blended learning, differentiation, and personalization in student learning. The creation of assessments that provide effective data, which is needed to create and sustain these learning environments, is where the coach can focus. This approach is a little less clinical, and starting from the practical need for implementing the different instructional practices can help keep teachers more excited at the prospect of assessing student learning than they would be to analyze student data.

ISTE STANDARDS FOR COACHES 6C. Partner with educators to empower students to use learning data to set their own goals and measure their progress.

Understanding and using data is not something only the teacher can learn. As the coach guides teachers to better understand how to collect and use their collected data to support student learning, they can also provide the teachers with resources and support for students to use data themselves. This can empower students not only to track their own progress, but to better understand how to set personal learning goals for themselves.

Professional Development Checklist

- [ ] Build a positive relationship with teachers, one that is non-evaluative and trusting.
- [ ] Research:
    - [ ] Block out time in the week to conduct research.
    - [ ] Adopt the attitude of "If I don't know it, I can find it for you."
- [ ] Co-planning:
    - [ ] Before co-planning, ask simple and relevant questions to help prepare for the co-planning meeting.
    - [ ] During co-planning, provide the teacher space to talk out thoughts and discuss successes and struggles.
    - [ ] During co-planning, stay focused on the goals established for the lesson or unit
    - [ ] After co-planning, offer additional support through modeling, co-teaching, observation, or reflection.
- [ ] Model:
    - [ ] Best instructional practices during professional learning
    - [ ] Lessons with students while the teacher observes
    - [ ] The implementation of technology and technology standards in lesson plans
    - [ ] What it is to be a life-long learner
    - [ ] Digital citizenship for teachers and students
- [ ] Co-teach:
    - [ ] When the lesson was co-planned
    - [ ] As a way to support the teacher with implementation of a new strategy
    - [ ] As a way to support the teacher with a learning experience that is larger th one teacher
- [ ] Data analysis and usage:
    - [ ] Situate data analysis and usage so it supports the instructional practices be implemented by teachers.

 **ISTE STANDARDS FOR COACHES 1C.** Cultivate a supportive coaching culture that encourages educators and leaders to achieve a shared vision and individual goals.

Coaching cycles can create a safe space for teachers to focus on growth goals (Kraft & Blazar, 2018). This is why it is so important that the educational technology coach is not an administrator or an evaluator of teachers. The coach needs to be able to build a relationship that is based on trust so the teacher and coach can be part of a collaborative partnership.

Educational technology coaches who use coaching cycles have often adapted those that were designed for other coaching roles. Literacy and instructional coaches have coaching cycles that can help to focus their support for teachers in a way that best meets their job's goals. Those cycles may not necessarily meet the need of educational technology coaches who are tasked with helping their staff to better utilize technology to support teaching and learning.

Popular Coaching Cycles and What Can Be Learned from Them

The Problem-Solving Cycle

The problem-solving cycle was introduced by Cathy A. Toll as a way for literacy coaches to help their teachers overcome barriers that prevent them from solving a particular problem of practice. This facilitative coaching cycle begins with a coaching conversation where the teacher identifies a problem, or "something that is getting in the way of the teacher's success" (Toll, 2016). This model's first phase (Problem) asks the coach to guide the teacher in identifying the goals for students and list all the barriers that stand in the way of reaching that goal. Once the barriers are identified and one is chosen as the priority to focus on, the partnership moves to the next phase (Understand) to better understand the problem. This is accomplished through a deep dive into the data that can help the team better understand what is causing the problem. With a clear understanding of the problem, in the third phase (Decide) the partnership can determine what to do to solve the problem. The team sets a clear and measurable

THE TRANSITION TO COACHING CYCLES

Nikita Porter, Technology and Learning Coach

"You should be a *coach*!" is what I kept hearing during the year I was asked to pilot a project-based learning (PBL) curriculum. It was an exciting year. My students were given a choice in how to present the solutions that their groups had created, observed, and proposed. Through that, the opportunity to explore tech tools and strategies continued to be the highlight of our units, and the fact that we had the time to be creative was an added plus.

As the year came to an end, an opportunity arose to be a technology and learning coach within my district. Entering this position, all new coaches were automatically enrolled in a coaching cohort. We were trained using the book *Peer Coaching* by Les Foltos. It provided in-depth training on how to question, rather than suggest, and to practice listening vs. talking.

After our sessions, I would return to my assigned school, where the routine of "Techie Thursday" or "Tech Tuesday" once-a-month meetings were well established. I began to see how difficult it was to implement a coaching cycle with individuals when group and team once-a-month meetings were already in place and expected. I also observed conversations and body language. I would hear "We *have* to go to a meeting." I would watch the timekeepers look for when it was time to leave to pick up their students, and occasionally I would hear "I wish we had more time to practice this stuff." Once, I received the dreadful "Do I have to go to your meeting because . . ." on a day that I had planned an exciting "Techie Thursday"—with prizes and all. I knew I had to make a change.

My assigned technology specialist would meet with me monthly to discuss my progress with coaching. I would share about the teachers using great strategies and tools that I observed or the ah-ha moments in my monthly meetings. I loved how she always knew where we had left off and would take notes and ask me questions that made me think of better ways I could support my teachers. She held me accountable for my ideas to ensure I acted on them. I realized how beneficial this was and how I would actually accomplish all of my goals as long as I knew she was coming and was going to ask me about my progress.

I took this and ran with it. It was a "coaching cycle!" Why hadn't I been doing this all along? *This* is what we have been trained to do. My monthly meetings worked for a very small percentage of teachers, and that wasn't effective, because the next month we had another topic and there was very little follow-up and follow-through in between. So before the year ended, I gave the teachers a heads-up that the following year would be different. I invited them in as teams, and each teacher completed a comfort, risk, and danger assessment via Google Forms so that I could create a coaching profile and know what each teacher was comfortable or not comfortable with, what motivated them, etc. Not all the questions were relevant, but those that weren't lightened the mood.

I rebranded myself, and in the next year began differentiated coaching—or at least that's what I called it. Teachers were asked to have a mandatory booking at the beginning of the year. During this meeting I suggested that they book me each month using an appointment scheduler. They *loved* it! Allowing them to share what they were excited about and not excited about, and asking questions that led to new discoveries and goals became a natural conversation. This was an opportunity to receive individual praise and encouragement. Teachers could plan with me, and I would follow up via email with templates for what we had discussed, then pop into their rooms and *see* implementation. They would tell me that our meetings were meaningful because the meetings were never on a topic they already knew about or didn't want to know about. I could tell when they needed to see me model something, and we would schedule it.

Documenting all this greatness is especially important. I used a template that would allow me to link any created docs, etc. and kept the goal for the year always in view so that we could see that our notes and next steps were evidence of achieving that goal. At the end of each session, I would incorporate our next meeting date into the document. I would reshare the document once I left the room and also share it again on the morning of our next meeting. In the "Next Steps" column, I would assign any tasks that I had promised to complete to myself using the @ symbol, plus my email address in Google Docs. This would generate an email reminder for myself.

Teachers will ask for examples or assistance, and if you forget, then you are seen as unreliable—or worse, as someone who makes the job harder. I knew it was important to always fulfill promises, and if I knew I couldn't do something, not to say that I could. I remained flexible. No one would get in "trouble" for cancelling, and I would send the link to reschedule in a friendly reminder email.

Did every teacher book me? No. However, the benefits from regular coaching cycles that were established outweighed any benefits from the type of coaching I had done in the past. It is simply a best practice to meet the needs of the individual teacher. We do it all the time for our students, right? Why not for our teachers and show them that we value their time—and increase productivity in the process?

As time progressed, my coaching relationships grew, and through word of mouth I would find myself with fewer booking slots available and having to book myself just to prep for my sessions and allow for follow-up and follow-through. The outcome? Teachers were excited about tech integration, and students were eager to learn more.

goal(s) for their work and brainstorms all the possible strategies to help them meet that goal(s). Once all possible strategies are laid out in front of the team, the teacher chooses which approach to try. In this fourth phase of the process (Try), the teacher works with the coach to identify what success looks like, then plan for the implementation and attempt to solve the problem using the identified strategy. Once the data is collected to help determine if the implementation was successful, the coach and teacher can go back to the Understand phase and continue the process until the problem has been solved (Toll, 2018).

Takeaways and Limitations of this Cycle for Edtech Coaches

The problem-solving cycle promotes the idea of using coaching cycles to solve problems of practice in a collaborative way. While edtech coaches can utilize their coaching cycle to solve problems, it is not always going to be the best approach for every coaching partnership because teachers may not have an instructional problem they have identified. They may already be using some fantastic instructional practices that get the job done and meet their students' learning goals, but they may still be able to better engage their students, enhance their activities, or extend the learning beyond the classroom through the use of technology-based pedagogies and resources (Kolb, 2017). The educational technology coach may observe a phenomenal lesson and still have suggestions that can move the strategies being used by the teacher beyond the lesson's current capabilities.

The Impact Cycle

Jim Knight is the creator of the Impact Cycle, an instructional coaching cycle that begins with the teacher and the coach taking time to identify where the instruction currently is by taking a deep and hard look at the instructional practices that are happening in the classroom. Together, they then determine where improvements can be made, set a goal to define those improvements, and identify an instructional practice that can help to meet that goal. The teacher is then taken through a process to learn about the chosen instructional practice that is further understood by having the practice modeled. Once the practice is learned, the focus becomes working to improve. The teacher and coach analyze data to assess the success of the instructional practice, determine if additional improvements need to be made, and plan the next steps (Knight, 2018).

Takeaways and Limitations of This Cycle for Edtech Coaches

The Impact Cycle is a great and thorough method for guiding teachers to improve instructional practices. The book itself, also called *The Impact Cycle*, is a great read for all coaches—regardless of their coaching concentration (instructional, literacy, math, edtech, etc.). It provides strategies and resources for each step in an easy-to-follow and usable way. Yet it cannot be taken as a whole and applied to educational technology coaches because it relies heavily on modeling and leaves out other key supports (described in chapter 4) that educational technology coaches can implement into their coaching cycle to improve practices through the utilization of technology-based pedagogies and resources.

Dynamic Learning Project: Digital Promise Coaching Model

Digital Promise launched a project that provided instructional coaches to fifty schools with the intention of determining the effect that coaching cycles would have on technology use and technology-based pedagogies used in the classroom. Schools were provided grants to hire an instructional coach who was trained to utilize coaching cycles and strategies with teachers in their school. The coaching cycle used had the coach and teacher identify challenges, investigate possible solutions, select which strategies to use, implement those strategies, and reflect on the lessons (Bakhshaei et al., 2018).

Takeaways and Limitations of This Cycle for Edtech Coaches

According to the Digital Promise report, the teachers who had a coach work through these cycles with them had increased use of technology and increased use of technology pedagogy. This cycle is reminiscent of the problem-solving cycle discussed earlier. The focus on strictly identifying challenges or problems limits the coaching to focusing on problems of practice or challenges. While no lesson is perfect, the focus for support from an educational technology coach does not have to solely focus on problems or challenges. The edtech coach can help the teacher take a fantastic lesson that has few to no challenges or problems and work with the teacher to further enhance the lesson, better engage students in the content, or extend that content beyond the classroom walls (Kolb, 2017).

Edtech Coaching Cycle

Edtech coaches need a coaching cycle that provides a structure that can keep the process effective while allowing the coaches to remain flexible enough to meet the technological and instructional needs of every teacher they work with.

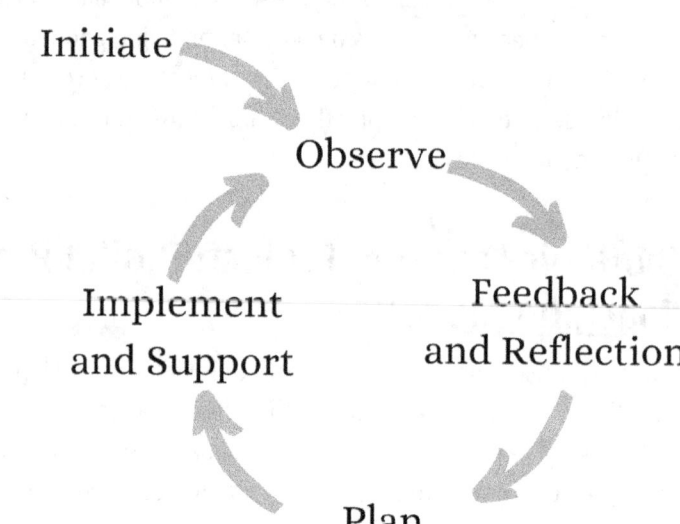

FIGURE 5.1 Visual depiction of the Edtech Coaching Cycle.

Initiate

There will be no growth or change in teaching practice if the teacher is not willing to be an active participant in the coaching cycle process. Making an individual participate in coaching cycles because an administrator is requiring it is not going to yield the type of results that are desired—and it wastes the resources of the educational technology coach. Participation in coaching cycles should be voluntary, as the teacher who is participating needs to have an open mind and a willingness to try new strategies and practices.

Getting the Right Participants

The first step is to gauge where teachers want to participate in the coaching cycle process. This can be done by sending out an interest form to teachers. Below is a possible example of such a form.

EDTECH COACHING
INTERST FORM

Educational Technology Coaching Interest Form

Name _____

How do you feel about participating in coaching cycles?

☐ I am interested in participating in coaching cycles now.

☐ I am interested in coaching cycles _____.
　　　　　　　　　　　　　　　　　　specific time of year or unit

☐ I may be interested later, please ask me again
　on _____.
　　　　　　date

☐ Not this semester.

Do you have a goal you would like to work on this year?

☐ Yes, I would like to work on _____.

☐ No, I would like feedback first.

The best days and times for me to meet are _____.

The Pre-Meeting

The pre-meeting provides an opportunity for the educational technology coach to discuss the teacher's goals for the coaching cycles and to help establish the norms and roles that the participants will play during the coaching cycles. Example information that can be gathered in this meeting includes:

- What are the communication preferences of the teacher?
    - How does the teacher want to receive feedback?
        - read the feedback via email or printed copy
        - go over the feedback together via meeting or video conference
        - hear the feedback asynchronously through a recording discussing the feedback to be watched or listened to alone
- How much time does the teacher need between receiving observational feedback and a post-conversation?
- Agree on the roles of each person.
    - The coach will:
        - provide observational feedback within twenty-four hours.
        - be present and focused during observations and meetings.
- The teacher will:
    - be present and focused during meetings.

This meeting may or may not end with an established growth goal. Some teachers may already know what they intend to get out of the coaching cycle, but others may not yet have a clear picture of where they would like to begin. The first observation and reflection may be necessary to help establish what goal(s) the teacher and coach will focus on. The meeting should end with a scheduled date for the first observation to take place.

Goal Setting

The goal for coaching can be set before or after the first observation. Consider discussing the teacher's professional learning goal that may have been established individually, with a PLC, or as a school and aligning the coaching goal(s) with it. Aligning these goals allows teachers to use the outcomes and any collaborations that result from the coaching cycles as evidence in their evaluation documents, if they choose.

ISTE STANDARDS FOR COACHES 2C. Establish shared goals with educators, reflect on successes, and continually improve coaching and teaching practice.

Observation

The intention of the observation is not to be evaluative but supportive, giving the educational technology coach an understanding of what the daily teaching and learning looks like while providing feedback to the teacher. Traditionally, an observation includes a physical visit to a classroom, but the observation could also be completed through a recording, livestream, or a visit to the teacher's learning management system. Each observation should be recorded through an observation feedback form that is shared with the teacher. Table 5.1 shares an example of such a form.

EDTECH COACHING OBSERVATION DOCUMENT

The form serves as a way to not only take notes, but also provide observational data and feedback to the teacher. While observing, be as concrete as possible. Describe what is seen and heard during the lesson, or what is seen and experienced as the learner going through the teacher's lesson in the learning management system. While the coaching focus does not always have to focus specifically on technology integration, taking notes about what and who is using the technology can provide insight into the current utilization of available tools and may prove to be invaluable information to the coach and teacher as they brainstorm action steps to meet established goals.

CHAPTER 5 • IMPLEMENTING FORMAL COACHING CYCLES

TABLE 5.1 Educational Technology Coaching Observation Form

TEACHER:	SUBJECT:	DATE:
COACH:	TOPIC:	TIME:

Current Coaching Goal:

Observation Notes:

I saw . . .

I heard . . .

I experienced . . .

Technology Integration Notes:

How was technology being used?

Who was the primary user of the technology?

Lesson Successes:

I was excited to see . . .

Questions I Have:

I wonder . . .

Reflection

After the observation form has been given to the teacher for review, the teacher should take time to reflect on the lesson and feedback. Providing teachers with a reflection protocol can help prevent them from becoming overwhelmed and also provide them with some guidance that can help them to think deeper about their lesson and teaching practice. One effective protocol for reflection is the "What? So what? Now what?" protocol. Below is an example document with focus questions for each of the steps for the protocol.

"WHAT? SO WHAT? NOW WHAT?" REFLECTION TOOL

What? So What? Now What?

Reflection Protocol

You do not have to answer every question in every section. Choose the questions that are most relevant to you and your thought process. You can also create questions for reflection.

What?

Describe what happened in the lesson.

- What were some successes in the lesson?
- What were some challenges in the lesson?
- What was the engagement level of the students to the lesson?
- What do you see in the observation feedback?

So What?

Describe the significance or impact.

- To what do you attribute these successes?
- Discuss the impact that the challenges had on the lesson.
- How did the student engagement affect their ability to meet learning goals?
- Describe your thoughts and reactions to the feedback.

Now What?

Describe what you would like to focus on next.

- What challenges would you like to address?
- What would you like to improve or learn?
- What changes might you make to the lesson if you were to present it again?

Adapted from: What? So what? Now what? Model designed by Rolfe et al (2001).

Plan

Once the teacher has had a chance to reflect on the feedback and practices, it is time to schedule a meeting to have a coaching conversation. This conversation should be scheduled as soon after the lesson as possible and result in action steps. These action steps should be small, measurable, and align with the coaching or professional learning goals set by the teacher. During the planning phase of the coaching cycle, the coach and

POST OBSERVATION AGENDA

teacher should go over the feedback and reflection, refocus on the goal for coaching, create a plan of action for the teacher, create a support plan for the coach, and schedule the next observation, if appropriate. Table 5.2 is a sample agenda for this meeting.

TABLE 5.2 Sample Post Observation Agenda

TIME ESTIMATE	FOCUS	NOTES
10 minutes	Teacher talks it out	
5 minutes	What I heard and saw	
5 minutes	Restate or create the goal	
10 minutes	What-ifs	
15 minutes	Create action plan	
15 minutes	Create support plan	
5 minutes	Schedule	

Teacher Talks It Out

To start the meeting, give teachers time and space to discuss the feedback they received and their reflection. Make sure to allow them to lead this discussion so they can talk about what they feel is important for them to focus on.

What I Heard and Saw

The coach should take this opportunity to restate the feedback and reflection takeaways the teacher just described while also adding anything else that may have been heard or seen by the coach during the observation.

Restate or Create the Goal

If a goal was not established prior to the observation, this is a good time to establish the overall goal for the coaching sessions. This could be finding a solution for a problem of practice; trying out a new instructional strategy; integrating technology to better enhance, engage, or extend learning for students; design an awesome learning experience for the classes' next lesson; personalize the learning environment; and so on.

What-Ifs

Once the goal is established or revisited, the coach and teacher can brainstorm a list of possible next steps. These should be bite-size tasks that can build on each other to move toward the goal.

Create Action Plan

The action plan is a timeline of next steps for the teacher. This should consist of only one or two steps or actions that can be implemented or accomplished prior to or during the next scheduled observation.

Create Support Plan

The support plan is a timeline and description of support the coach will provide to the teacher. This can include any of the supports described in chapter 4.

Schedule

The meeting should end with a clear timeline that includes the date and time of the next observation (if desired).

Implement and Support

With a plan of action and a plan of support, the teacher and coach can take the next steps toward meeting the established goal. The teacher can implement the action plan while the coach provides one or more of the supports described in depth in chapter 4, including research, modeling, co-planning, or co-teaching. As the implementation comes to a close, the partnership should look at scheduling another observation to provide an opportunity for feedback and reflection that can provide understanding around the effectiveness of the implementation and support.

The Timing of It All

Some coaching cycles are extremely specific on the time frame in which each stage of the coaching cycle should be implemented. In the case of the edtech coaching cycle, a strict time frame for each stage is not recommended because teachers are going to need different timelines according to their chosen actions and their level of comfort to move forward with—or without—certain supports.

A technologically strong teacher whose action step is to try a new collaborative technology might only need research support and a technology tool suggestion from the coach. That teacher may take, learn, and utilize that resource on their own, meaning the coach would only provide the suggestion and show up to observe the next scheduled lesson where the tool is being used by students.

Another teacher may want to explore the use of a new instructional strategy that not only requires the research support of the educational technology coach, but also co-planning and co-teaching of the lesson where the strategy is being used the first time. This cycle would take longer to conclude, as the implementation-and-support stage in this example could take weeks to complete.

The timeline for the coaching cycle should be organic and move at the pace the teacher is comfortable with. Pushing teachers too much may cause them to become overwhelmed and make them want to disengage from the process completely. The idea of the coaching cycle is to provide feedback and support, not extra stress or work for the teacher.

Formal Coaching Cycles Checklist

- [ ] Initiate:
  - [ ] Share the intentions of the coaching cycle with teachers and determine who is interested in participating.
  - [ ] Meet prior to the first observation to discuss possible goals for coaching and establish roles for the teacher and coach.
- [ ] Observe:
  - [ ] Collect observational data that focuses on what is seen or heard.
- [ ] Provide feedback and time for reflection:
  - [ ] Present feedback through the teacher's chosen method in a timely manner.
  - [ ] Provide time for the teacher to reflect on the feedback, along with the teaching and learning that were observed.
- [ ] Plan:
  - [ ] Create an action plan of bite-size next steps for the teacher.
  - [ ] Create a support plan that provides the best supports for the teacher's action plan.
  - [ ] Create a timeline of events.
- [ ] Implement and support:
  - [ ] Support teachers during implementation of the action plan.
- [ ] Keep the coaching cycle on an organic timeline that makes sense for the teacher.

6

FOCUSED LEADERSHIP RESPONSIBILITIES

Many edtech coaches tend to get pulled into various leadership tasks that can prevent them from providing the coaching and support described in chapters 3, 4, and 5. Covering administrative duties, serving as a testing coordinator, maintaining student data, providing extensive technology support, and teaching regularly scheduled courses are some of the responsibilities often placed on edtech coaches. Not only does having these roles placed on the edtech coach make it harder to provide support, it also changes the way teachers relate to the coach.

Finding a Leadership Niche

While pulling the edtech coach away from administrative and technology break/fix roles, there are plenty of places where the coach can provide leadership within the school and in the district. This will look different for every school and every coach because each school community has their own needs and each coach has individualized strengths. Finding the niche for the coach to fill begins with determining the needs of the school. Is there a need to deepen student interest in STEM or STEAM? Does the school need a student technology support center? Should there be additional guidance and resources created for embedding the ISTE Standards for Students into learning? Is there a need for a school data team, and would the edtech be a good fit to lead this team?

Whatever the chosen leadership opportunity or opportunities happen to be, there are some steps the educational technology coach can make to ensure work in this area is continuing to provide growth within the school or district.

Projects and Programs

I currently work with edtech coaches from the district level. Each year, the coaches I lead break into small teams designed to create district-level plans, solve problems through the completion of a project, and work on establishing or maintaining programs. My teams are made up of four individuals (not because of any rule, but because teams of four make an even split in my district) who are asked to focus on the assignments we as a team have agreed needs to have priority. Our teams have tackled the creation of a district technology plan, the creation of training and materials for getting teachers to utilize #GoOpen resources, designing a plan for implementing appropriate computer skills at specific grade levels, developing a procedure for evaluating educational technology resources to ensure they meet privacy policy standards, and maintaining a choice professional learning database for teachers to participate in professional development beyond what is provided within the schools.

THE RIGHT PROJECT WITH THE RIGHT PEOPLE

Holly King, Instructional Technology Facilitator

As an educational technology coach, my role has two critical components: building relationships with the educators you serve and identifying the instructional needs of your environment to inform, create, and implement professional learning opportunities and support to ensure continued growth for all learners. In my tenure as a teacher leader—and now, as an educational technology coach—I recognize that the ingredient to success in this role lies in the congruence of these two components with the building/district vision. Educators who can identify instructional needs and can transform those needs into intentional professional learning that is tightly aligned to student growth and district goals are perfect candidates for educational technology coach positions. In fact, this describes my path.

As a teacher leader in my building, I recognized a need for professional learning in instructional technology, so I drafted a vision of what this could look like and pitched my idea to my leadership team. In a brainstorming session with a collaborative leadership team that was open to my ideas, I learned more about what they had identified as an instructional need for the teachers in the building. Armed with a huge whiteboard and multicolored markers, an integrated professional learning plan emerged that tied instructional strategies and technology tools that all centered around the instructional topic of rigor.

For nine months, we—the leadership duo and I—planned opportunities to showcase exceptional learning environments through learning walks, wove professional learning into professional learning communities and faculty meetings by modeling best practices to deliver content, provided asynchronous learning modules that combined instructional practices with technology tools, and ensured that support was available to teachers who were ready to take instructional risks. For nine months, we celebrated teachers who tried new things, connected teachers to encourage instructional partnerships, and watched our classrooms transform into highly engaging learning environments.

District leaders took notice of the shift in energy in our building, and they opened a space for my voice in professional learning at the district level. The first question was, How could we take our work in our building and scale it to the benefit of all teachers in our district? Leveraging the work of other district leaders in the establishment of an "innovative teachers" cohort, I turned to this group of teacher leaders to bring my vision into reality. In five months (many during our summer vacation), we used monthly coffee dates, emails, and digital platforms to build twelve asynchronous, highly engaging professional learning courses that integrated instructional practices and technology tools. In addition, these courses were tightly aligned to our district's educational vision, as well as to our educator evaluation tool, digital technology standards, and National Board standards. In addition to teachers learning in a collaborative space across multiple buildings, teachers walked away with an artifact that demonstrated growth that could be used to support their annual summative evaluation.

A team of ten teachers—educational leaders without titles—built the foundation of professional learning in our district that continues today. Spanning buildings, grade levels, subjects, and roles, this group of twelve teachers craft teacher leaders by encouraging others to take risks in their classrooms, sharing instructional strategies with colleagues, and most recently, presenting their strategies to larger audiences through district webinars. As edtech coaches, we are instructional partners helping others develop their own visions and bring them to fruition while serving as a practice partner—or even a wingman—during implementation.

As I have demonstrated in my work at the building, district, and state levels, educational technology coaches are the fast-paced implementers, the doers, on your team. When given a seat at the table, these leaders will transform educational visions into a reality. By connecting ideas and embracing the strengths of the people with those ideas, they support an institutional change from within the organization, which is both faster and more sustainable than other methods. If you are in a leadership position in your organization, I urge you to carve a space for your educational technology coach on your leadership team.

Educational technology coaches are not limited to providing such leadership at the district level. These types of leadership tasks can also be taken on at the school level. As an edtech coach, I was given the opportunity to provide leadership for our school's data team. The team was tasked with researching, designing, and helping to implement a school-wide data analysis plan to be used to better analyze student data. This aligned with the standards for my educational technology coaching role and met a need that was identified at my school. I have seen other technology coaches take on STEAM or STEM programs, coding clubs, lead a media and technology advisory committee (MTAC), and take on the design and implementation of various school-wide initiatives.

Identifying the Work

Beginning this work starts with identifying what the work is. Projects and programs are different beasts. A project is intended to be a set of tasks that has a final goal or outcome. Projects could include:

- Designing teacher resources for a particular topic
- The creation of a formal process or policy
- Creating a district or school-wide plan, such as a:
    - district technology plan
    - school technology plan
    - school improvement plan

Unlike projects, programs do not end. They are established to provide for an ongoing need within the school or district. Examples include:

- Establishing and maintaining a STEAM or STEM program
- Creating and maintaining a student organization
- Implementing and evaluating a district- or school-wide plan, such as a:
    - district technology plan
    - school technology plan
    - school improvement plan

Knowing what is being worked on helps to determine the scope of the work and the amount of time that will need to be put into the tasks surrounding it. This helps the edtech coach and administration determine if leading up this particular plan, project, or program is realistic because taking on one or more of these leadership roles should not take up so much time during the working day that it hinders the coach from providing formal professional learning, personalized support, or formal coaching cycles to teachers. It is better to spread such leadership opportunities out among leaders throughout the school than to place too much on the edtech coach.

Organizing the Work

To help my small teams understand the time they will need to commit to their identified leadership responsibility, we take on a project planning mentality. For anyone who has completed a project with formal project planning documentation and techniques, you know how useful it is to establish the goals of the project, plan out the tasks, and set milestones that are aligned with realistic dates for completion. I strongly encourage any educational technology coach to pick up a project management book and become familiar with the formal process of managing large projects. However, I have found that with many of the projects taken on in this role, many of the formal steps may not be necessary for every project. So I have created some simplified documents that my edtech coaches use when they work in their small project teams.

Even if the team is focused on a program, I have them follow these project planning steps to keep them focused on the milestones and tasks needed to be completed throughout the year. It gives our whole team a predictable protocol to follow so every small team's work is easily followed by other teams when we come together to provide feedback throughout the year. Because the materials presented below can be used with both projects and program planning, the documents are just titled "project." For programs, substitute the word "program" for "project."

To get started, the team meets and establishes the focus, members of the team, description of the project, goals, a description of the final product, and a list of milestones that need to be met within the project. You can use the project plan brainstorm document (accessible by QR code) shown in Figure 6.1.

PROJECT PLAN
BRAINSTORM

Project Plan Brainstorm

Focus: (Title of the project)

Team Members: (Names of team members)

Description: (Description of the purpose for the project)

Goals:

Final Product: (What does "finished" look like?)

Milestones:

MILESTONE	TASKS TO COMPLETE TO REACH THIS MILESTONE

FIGURE 6.1 Project plan brainstorm document.

Once the initial brainstorming is complete, further details need to be fleshed out so individual tasks can be identified, dates for tasks to be completed need to be set, and the responsible person for each task needs to be identified. To help organize this information, I like to use a spreadsheet that provides drop-down menus to help identify at a glance where the team is with each task.

PROJECT PLAN SPREADSHEET

Milestone	Description of Task	Category	Goal Dates	Status
Project Brainstorming	Branstorming Meeting	Meeting	9/15/2021	Scheduled
Project Brainstorming	Complete Brainstorming Document and Get Agreement from Team	Deadline	9/16/2021	In Progress
Project Brainstorming	Get the Project Overview to the Director	Communication	9/17/2021	Not Started

FIGURE 6.2 Example project plan spreadsheet.

Gathering Feedback

Breaking our larger team into these smaller focused groups allowed for more of these initiatives to be worked on simultaneously and provided a built-in support system for sharing out and gathering feedback. At any district-level PLC meeting, the smaller teams were able to share out where they were with their work and gather feedback from their peers. Regardless of whether the edtech coach is working on a district- or school-based project or program, there needs to be built-in feedback that is available to the coach. This can be done with a district PLC, like in our example, with a group of school leaders, or with a self-established PLC from across the globe.

Feedback is an important element in growth. The growth and success of the project or program can be drastically enhanced when feedback is available throughout the process. When our teams provide feedback to each other, each team takes turns presenting their goals, where they are within their project plan, and how they envision the final product to look (if there is a final product). The other teams provide feedback according to a simple form, show in Table 6.2.

PROJECT FEEDBACK DOCUMENT

While the educational technology coach's primary focus should be on the direct support of their teachers as they integrate digital teaching and learning pedagogies, the utilization of this individual for school or district projects or programs allows the coach to lead system-wide changes that affect their community.

TABLE 6.2 Project Feedback Form

	PROJECT FEEDBACK FORM		
	I HEARD/I SAW . . .	I WONDER . . .	I SUGGEST . . .
EXAMPLE	I heard the team will be responsible for reviewing these requests.	I wonder how the team will know when a request comes in for review?	I suggest having the spreadsheet send an email alert when there are changes.
COMMENT 1			
COMMENT 2			
COMMENT 3			

Focused Leadership Checklist

- [ ] Find a need or a niche that can be filled by the edtech coach.
    - [ ] Should align with the coach's skills
    - [ ] Should not get in the way of providing professional learning, personalized support, or coaching cycles to teachers
- [ ] Determine if the leadership opportunity is a project or program.
- [ ] Define the goals and actions to complete the project or move the program forward.
- [ ] Organize the actions according to the date they will need to be completed.
- [ ] Plan for and use feedback to make the project or program even better.

7

PUTTING IT ALL TOGETHER

In the prior chapters, there are a lot of activities, tasks, meetings, and responsibilities described for the educational technology coach. Keeping all of these supports available while also allowing time for research, planning, and other tasks that land on the edtech coach on a daily basis can be quite the balancing act. It is easy to get pulled out of the coaching cycles and away from the research and planning to fix broken devices, set up software and web applications, or maintain technology inventory. To prevent being pulled in a million different directions all day, there are a few tricks the coach can employ:

1. Let priorities and support services be known.
2. Remember the ten-minute rule.
3. Know the rhythm of the school.
4. Be transparent with the schedule.
5. Book yourself.

Let Priorities and Support Services Be Known

The start of the school year is always a great time to reset and refresh. The first days provide a perfect opportunity coaches to reintroduce themselves and their services to the staff. To start, coaches can provide a one-page infographic or menu of services that they provide (Figure 7.1). This gives teachers a reference point for understanding what the coach's role is and how it can support their work in the classroom.

Edtech Coaching Services

Personalized Support

Research
Let me help you research the most effective edtech tools and strategies that will help meet student learning outcomes.

Co-Planning
I can provide support in helping to reimagine a lesson you may have used before, or I can help you plan something brand new.

Co-Teaching
Whether you are planning a big lesson, unit, project, or just want support testing out a new strategy, I can come into your classes to help team teach any subject.

Data Support
Let's work together to utilize student data. I am available to help create assessment resources and deep-dive into the data with you.

Professional Learning Sessions
Professional learning opportunities will be available throughout the year. Yet, you don't have to wait for the topic you want to show up on any schedule. Let me know what you are interested in learning more about and we can dive into the topic together. I can work with you 1:1 or with any PLC as a group.

Coaching Cycles
Coaching cycles allow us to work together on implementing new strategies and solving daily classroom problems. This approach brings me into your classroom to provide feedback and personalized supports tailored to your individualized professional goals.

Contact Me:
Email:
Phone:
Calendar:

FIGURE 7.1 Example of a coaching menu.

Remember the Ten-Minute Rule

Notice that the services listed above do not include fixing broken technology, which is arguably the most common activity that coaches get pulled into, taking time from their ability to provide coaching and support to teachers. Let's be clear: the educational technology coach is *not* the person who should be maintaining technology systems or troubleshooting hardware or software that isn't working. Yet school budgets may not allow for both an educational technology coach and a technician to be on-site every day. This means that the edtech coach often serves as the first line of defense for technical problems.

One strategy to help prevent too much time loss when the coach has to look at a technical problem is the ten-minute rule. If the edtech coach is asked to fix a hardware or application problem and it takes more than ten minutes to determine the solution to the problem, then it's time to put in a help desk ticket for the school's technician to take over. From there, the focus of the conversation becomes, "What can I help you with *instructionally* to keep your class going in the right direction until technical support can fix the issue?" Figure 7.2. shows a flow chart demonstrating how this process can go.

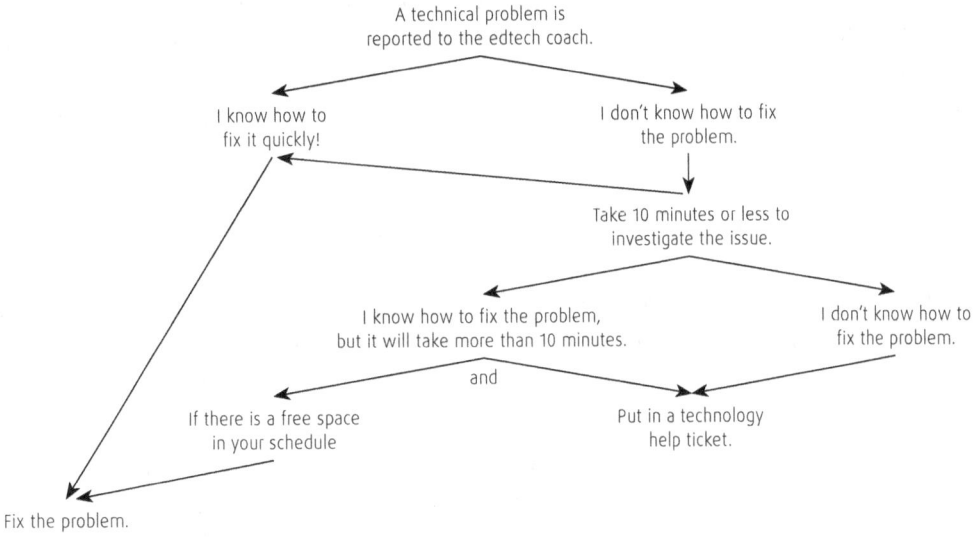

FIGURE 7.2 Technical support decision tree.

Notice that if the edtech coach can fix the problem quickly or if there is time that can be scheduled to fix it, then it is okay to fix the problem. The trick is not to fix a technical issue *at the expense* of meeting other support obligations. Say that the technology coach knows how to fix the problem, but it will take twenty to thirty minutes and she is scheduled to be in a classroom co-teaching in fifteen minutes. The coach should put in a ticket for technical support and get ready to co-teach. If time is available in her schedule later, she can fix the issue and close out the technical support ticket—only if she is able to get to it before support arrives.

Teachers should be aware from the very first day that this is the process for technical support problems, but to be honest there are a couple of times in the year where this rule may need to be broken. For instance, the first week of school is often one of the roughest weeks for technical issues. With hardware having sat for weeks or months without being used, deep cleaning that required everything to be unplugged and moved, and new staff who are not familiar with their classroom setup, it is hard to stick to the ten-minute rule. For a week or two before the edtech coach can jump into the main coaching and support responsibilities, in most instances they will need to support teachers as those teachers set up and build their understanding of how to get their technology going. The week after a major break or a large transition, such as what was seen during the COVID-19 pandemic, where teachers and students moved from face-to-face learning to remote, then back again, may also require an exception to this rule. But once the students are in, devices are all checked out, and the school year is up and running, then the ten-minute rule can be applied with more fidelity.

Know the Rhythm of the School

With the exception of the first couple weeks of a new school year, the day or two after coming back from a long break, and the last two weeks of the school year, school days often have a particular rhythm to them. Edtech coaches can feel this out the first few weeks and make sure their schedule aligns. As a former coach, I would make sure I was one of the first people in the school building because the requests and quick-fix problems tended to come in the morning and any afternoon issues were often not reported, as they seemed to be okay to put on hold until the following morning. Knowing this, I would arrive early to make myself available and walk the halls to provide any early morning support teachers needed. I also kept up with teacher planning periods so I could make sure that if I had an open schedule, I could walk the halls and pop in on teachers. It was amazing the number of requests for support I would get just stopping in to check in on people. They would often say things like, "Oh, I've been meaning to email you. Can you help me with . . . ?" Knowing school and teacher schedules, and understanding the times of the day where most of the problems arise or when teachers are free to have relationship-building conversations, can make a big difference in what supports the coach is asked to provide and for whom.

Be Transparent with the Schedule

Scheduling times with teachers can get tricky. While most everyone in a school has a strict time schedule, the edtech coach does not and needs to be able to provide services around everyone else's open time slots. Most teachers have relatively short time spans in which they are not scheduled to be working directly with students. Planning, grading, paperwork, student meetings, PLCs, and a number of other responsibilities compete for this time. One of the least effective strategies for scheduling is the back-and-forth-email method. This is where the coach and teacher suggest times and days of a support meeting by emailing each other back and forth multiple times before they finally land on when to meet.

While face-to-face, the coach and teacher can easily compare schedules and decide on a time, but this isn't always feasible, especially in a larger school or, as in the case of COVID-19, when everyone is working remotely. The best solution I have found is to share my live calendar with everyone. If the school uses Google, it is as simple as allowing everyone viewing access. If the coach prefers not to share the calendar directly, there are a number of sites and services that can share available times so teachers can see when the coach is able to meet. These services allow for individuals to schedule a time that meets their availability and reschedule if a conflict arises later. Schedule transparency and providing teachers the ability to schedule the coach without the need for back-and-forth emails or tracking the coach down to determine the best times can help teachers who are swamped and have the highest need for support to quickly request it without too many extra steps.

A short list of applications that can do this can be found at **edtechcoachingprimer.com**.

Book Yourself

Planning PD, researching for teachers, preparing materials for a co-teaching or modeling session—these are all tasks that require some time to sit and do. Often, edtech coaches can get so caught up in the day-to-day support and relationship-building activities that they end up doing all of their desk work after hours. This is not a new problem, as teachers, administrators, and most roles in education tend to do work after hours. Yet it isn't healthy for this to be the normal operating procedure. Leaving desk work and research to after hours every single week is draining and can lead to burnout. It is okay for coaches to book themselves an hour here or there to get their tasks completed. In the example schedule shown in Figure 7.3, notice that there are a couple of slots for planning and focused research:

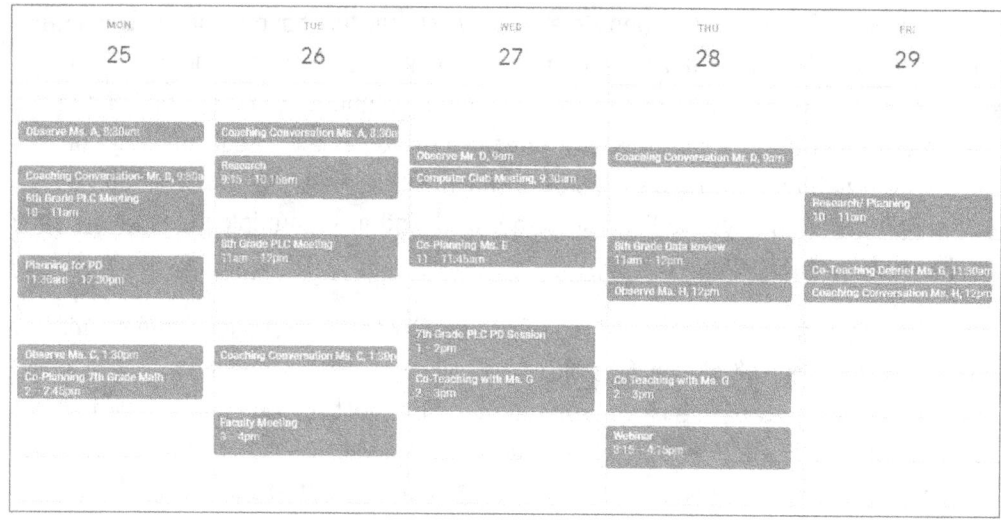

FIGURE 7.3 Example of a weeklong edtech coaching calendar.

Time is a precious commodity for everyone. By providing a clear understanding of what the coach is able to do to support teachers, limiting the amount of time spent on tasks that will take away from the most impactful work the edtech coach does, understanding the schedules of the individuals being served, and being transparent with their schedule, the edtech coach can be more effective and intentional with the time available during the school day. The intent is to be present, be flexible, and be ready to support teachers.

Putting It All Together Checklist

- [ ] Be clear with supports.
  - [ ] Provide an infographic or menu of services.
  - [ ] Share and stick to your process for assessing what you can and cannot fix (ten-minute rule).
- [ ] Know the daily rhythm of the school.
  - [ ] Use your unplanned time wisely by:
    - [ ] being proactive about common times you will be needed
    - [ ] checking in on teachers
- [ ] Be transparent with your time.
  - [ ] Share your calendar.
  - [ ] Provide a way for teachers to easily schedule meetings.
  - [ ] Book yourself so you can get *your* tasks done too.

8

REFLECTING AND PLANNING FOR PERSONAL GROWTH AS A COACH

If you are a coach reading this book, you may be at the point of asking, "Where do I start?" Before jumping into how to schedule these coaching tasks, let's take some time for you to evaluate where you are with the ISTE Standards for Coaches. The self-evaluation form shared in Table 8.1 can be used as a year-to-year measure of how you are meeting these standards. Be honest with yourself and know that it is okay to be proficient or to need improvement in an area—or even many areas. The intention of this document is to refocus you on the ISTE Standards for Coaches and keep these standards as a guide for your work. There is a rating for each standard, followed by two questions. The rating terms are:

- ✖ **Leads Others:** The coach does this above and beyond expectations and is seen as a leader to others in this area. This may mean the coach is the go-to person for the PLC, provides PD to other coaches, or has written on the topic for publication.
- ✖ **Exceptional:** The coach does this above and beyond expectations.
- ✖ **Proficient:** The coach does this well, meeting expectations.
- ✖ **Needs Improvement:** The coach isn't meeting this standard as expected.
- ✖ **Not Applicable:** The coach cannot meet this standard in the current environment. (There may be hurdles that need to be addressed before the coach is expected to meet this standard.)

Two considerations you should make are:

1. Describe the rationale for choosing the ratings above. This is intended to give you space to describe why you rated yourself as you did. It is also a good place to provide examples of where you provide leadership or explain why you feel you need improvement when looking at these particular standards.

2. What hurdles do you face to meet this standard? This question is intended to provide you a place to describe the things that could be preventing you from meeting this standard in a way you would like—for example, a scheduling conflict you have, a problem with the way your role is perceived by teachers or administration, or any other number of things. Identifying hurdles may seem like just a place to complain, but if you are able to identify them, you can begin to brainstorm how to address them so you can meet those standards in the future. Some hurdles will be out of your control, but recognizing that is important too.

ISTE STANDARDS FOR COACHES (2019) SELF-EVALUATION SHEET

TABLE 8.1 ISTE Standards for Coaches Self-Evaluation

CHANGE AGENT. Coaches inspire educators and leaders to use technology to create equitable and ongoing access to high-quality learning.

COACHES:	LEADS OTHERS	EXCEPTIONAL	PROFICIENT	NEEDS IMPROVEMENT	NOT APPLICABLE
a. Create a shared vision and culture for using technology to learn and accelerate transformation through the coaching process.					
b. Facilitate equitable use of digital learning tools and content that meet the needs of each learner.					
c. Cultivate a supportive coaching culture that encourages educators and leaders to achieve a shared vision and individual goals.					
d. Recognize educators across the organization who use technology effectively to enable high-impact teaching and learning.					
e. Connect leaders, educators, instructional support, technical support, domain experts, and solution providers to maximize the potential of technology for learning.					

Describe your rationale for the ratings chosen above:

What hurdles do you face to meet this standard? :

CONNECTED LEARNER. Coaches model the ISTE Standards for Students and the ISTE Standards for Educators and identify ways to improve their coaching practice.

COACHES:	LEADS OTHERS	EXCEPTIONAL	PROFICIENT	NEEDS IMPROVEMENT	NOT APPLICABLE
a. Pursue professional learning that deepens expertise in the ISTE Standards in order to serve as a model for educators and leaders.					

b. Actively participate in professional learning networks to enhance coaching practice and keep current with emerging technology and innovations in pedagogy and the learning sciences.

c. Establish shared goals with educators, reflect on successes and continually improve coaching and teaching practice.

Describe your rationale for the ratings chosen above:

What hurdles do you face to meet this standard? :

COLLABORATOR. Coaches establish productive relationships with educators in order to improve instructional practice and learning outcomes.

COACHES:	LEADS OTHERS	EXCEPTIONAL	PROFICIENT	NEEDS IMPROVEMENT	NOT APPLICABLE
a. Establish trusting and respectful coaching relationships that encourage educators to explore new instructional strategies.					
b. Partner with educators to identify digital learning content that is culturally relevant, developmentally appropriate, and aligned to content standards.					
c. Partner with educators to evaluate the efficacy of digital learning content and tools to inform procurement decisions and adoption.					
d. Personalize support for educators by planning and modeling the effective use of technology to improve student learning.					

Describe your rationale for the ratings chosen above:

What hurdles do you face to meet this standard? :

continued

LEARNING DESIGNER. Coaches model and support educators to design learning experiences and environments to meet the needs and interests of all students.

COACHES:	LEADS OTHERS	EXCEPTIONAL	PROFICIENT	NEEDS IMPROVEMENT	NOT APPLICABLE
a. Collaborate with educators to develop authentic, active learning experiences that foster student agency, deepen content mastery, and allow students to demonstrate their competency.					
b. Help educators use digital tools to create effective assessments that provide timely feedback and support personalized learning.					
c. Collaborate with educators to design accessible and active digital learning environments that accommodate learner variability.					
d. Model the use of instructional design principles with educators to create effective digital learning environments.					

Describe your rationale for the ratings chosen above:

What hurdles do you face to meet this standard? :

PROFESSIONAL LEARNING FACILITATOR. Coaches plan, provide, and evaluate the impact of professional learning for educators and leaders to use technology to advance teaching and learning.

COACHES:	LEADS OTHERS	EXCEPTIONAL	PROFICIENT	NEEDS IMPROVEMENT	NOT APPLICABLE
a. Design professional learning based on needs assessments and frameworks for working with adults to support their cultural, social-emotional, and learning needs.					

b. Build the capacity of educators, leaders, and instructional teams to put the ISTE Standards into practice by facilitating active learning and providing meaningful feedback.

c. Evaluate impact of professional learning and continually make improvements in order to meet school-wide vision for using technology for high-impact teaching and learning.

Describe your rationale for the ratings chosen above:

What hurdles do you face to meet this standard? :

DATA-DRIVEN DECISION-MAKER. Coaches model and support the use of qualitative and quantitative data to inform their own instruction and professional learning.

COACHES:	LEADS OTHERS	EXCEPTIONAL	PROFICIENT	NEEDS IMPROVEMENT	NOT APPLICABLE
a. Assist educators and leaders in securely collecting and analyzing student data.					
b. Support educators to interpret qualitative and quantitative data to inform their decisions and support individual student learning.					
c. Partner with educators to empower students to use learning data to set their own goals and measure their progress.					

Describe your rationale for the ratings chosen above:

What hurdles do you face to meet this standard? :

continued

CHAPTER 8 • REFLECTING AND PLANNING FOR PERSONAL GROWTH AS A COACH

DIGITAL CITIZEN ADVOCATE. Coaches model digital citizenship and support educators and students in recognizing the responsibilities and opportunities inherent in living in a digital world.

COACHES:	LEADS OTHERS	EXCEPTIONAL	PROFICIENT	NEEDS IMPROVEMENT	NOT APPLICABLE
a. Inspire and encourage educators and students to use technology for civic engagement and to address challenges to improve their communities.					
b. Partner with educators, leaders, students and families to foster a culture of respectful online interactions and a healthy balance in their use of technology.					
c. Support educators and students to critically examine the sources of online media and identify underlying assumptions.					
d. Empower educators, leaders, and students to make informed decisions to protect their personal data and curate the digital profile they intend to reflect.					

Describe your rationale for the ratings chosen above:

What hurdles do you face to meet this standard? :

The ISTE Standards for Coaches self-evaluation sheet is a good way to measure growth from year to year, but when framing those goals into some specific and actionable tasks that focus on the four primary areas of the edtech coaching role, you need to focus on the strengths you bring to your position and the way you can use those strengths to work with your teachers. You can use the reflection document shared in Table 8.2 to look at each of the four areas of the edtech coaching role and think through the actions you can take within your role to meet the ISTE Standards for Coaches. Whether you are a first-year or tenth-year coach, taking some time to think through this can help you with your own personal goal setting for the year. Keep in mind that as you identify your goal or goals for the year, they need to be attainable. Try not to overburden yourself with too many. Also keep in mind that you want to have the chance to dig deep into the ISTE Standard or Standards that you are going to focus on.

EDTECH COACHING REFLECTION DOCUMENT

TABLE 8.2 Edtech Coaching Reflection Form

COACH:	DATE:
PROFESSIONAL DEVELOPMENT	
Strengths: 1. 2. 3.	Examples of prior work that demonstrate these strengths: 1. 2. 3.
PERSONALIZED SUPPORT	
Strengths: 1. 2. 3.	Examples of prior work that demonstrate these strengths: 1. 2. 3.
FORMAL COACHING CYCLES	
Strengths: 1. 2. 3.	Examples of prior work that demonstrate these strengths: 1. 2. 3.
LEADERSHIP	
Strengths: 1. 2. 3.	Examples of prior work that demonstrate these strengths: 1. 2. 3.
GROWTH GOAL(S)	
Area(s) for Improvement:	How will this be measured?:

Describe what you would like to do to promote this growth:

The ISTE Standard(s) for Coaches that I will focus on is/are:

With your goal(s) identified, you can set a plan to begin working toward them. This can be accomplished through independent research and self-study, taking a course or working toward a certification, attending conferences, taking part in coaching cycles of your own, or participating in your extended PLC. Consider setting a month-by-month plan for yourself, much like what was discussed for teacher professional learning in chapter 3. Table 8.3 gives an example of how you can adapt the PD schedule to meet your needs and keep you on target.

EDTECH COACHING PROFESSIONAL LEARNING PLAN

ISTE STANDARDS FOR COACHES 2A. Pursue professional learning that deepens expertise in the ISTE Standards in order to serve as a model for educators and leaders.

TABLE 8.3 Edtech Coaching Professional Learning Plan

GOAL FOR PROFESSIONAL LEARNING: Add your goal(s) here

MONTH	TOPIC	ACTIVITY	MATERIALS	DATE COMPLETE
AUG.	Self-Assessment and Goal-Setting	Complete ISTE Standards for Coaches (2019) Self-Evaluation Sheet and the Edtech Coaching Reflection	• ISTE Standards for Coaches (2019) Self-Evaluation Sheet • Edtech Coaching Reflection	
SEPT.				
OCT.				
NOV.				
DEC.				
JAN.				
FEB.				
MAR.				
APR.				
MAY				

Some edtech coaches are left to ensure they get their needed professional development themselves, while others may have some guidance provided to them by their school or district. Either way, keeping yourself growing professionally is an important part of making sure you are ready to meet the needs of your teachers. Make sure to set aside professional learning time each month for yourself. It does not have to look the same each time or be a part of a particular program, but it should meet your own growth needs.

Reflecting and Planning for Personal Growth as a Coach Checklist

- [ ] Refocus yourself on the ISTE Standards for Coaches.
- [ ] Reflect on your current strengths and determine what goal or goals you would like to focus on for growth (make sure it is a goal you can accomplish in a given time period).
- [ ] Create a personal plan for your professional learning and share it with your administration.
- [ ] It is okay to provide time for your own growth!

9

HIRING AND SUPPORTING THE EDTECH COACH

Unlike chapter 8, which is directly written for the edtech coach, there is no way to know exactly who to address here. The leader who supports the edtech coach could be a superintendent, principal, chief technology officer, or director. Whatever the title, one of these administrators is probably tasked in some form or fashion to hire, support, and/or evaluate the edtech coach. So this will be written with the assumption that I am writing to an audience who does those things or would be tasked to do those things if their district or school is considering adding this role.

Start with a Job Description

As discussed in chapter 1, the edtech coaching role is often misunderstood and misused. The first step in getting stakeholders and potential coaches to understand the focus of this role is to write out a clear job description that provides everyone with a reference point for tasks. Below is an example of job description statements that can be used or altered as needed to ensure that additional district and school needs are met.

EXAMPLE JOB DESCRIPTION

Example Job Description

In _____ school, our educational technology coach is expected to work in alignment with the ISTE Standards for Coaches and is responsible for:

- remaining up to date on emerging technologies and instructional practices
- establishing and leading a school-wide vision of technology usage that promotes equity, enables high-impact teaching and learning, and is aligned with the strategic plan for the school
- facilitating professional learning that focuses on the school's vision for digital teaching and learning, along with the needs of the teachers, and is aligned with the ISTE Standards for Educators
- providing personalized support to teachers through research, co-planning, co-teaching, and modeling
- supporting teachers in the collection and analysis of data that can drive classroom instruction focused on student need
- providing feedback and support through a formalized coaching cycle
- supporting teachers in the creation and implementation of lessons that align with curricular standards, as well as the ISTE Standards for Students
- modeling positive digital citizenship for teachers and students
- assisting in the evaluation and selection of digital teaching and learning resources
- providing limited Tier 1 support for maintaining school-based technology

Finding the Right Person

With the description in place, a clear vision of what this individual will need to do is established and the search for the right person can begin. Finding the right person to fill the edtech coaching role can be a daunting task. The individual who fills this role needs to be a strong instructional leader who is able to relate to the teachers that the coach will serve. It is useful if the coach has been a classroom teacher before, as teachers may find it hard to take feedback or trust the supports that are being provided to them by the coach if the coach has not had experience as a classroom teacher. This person needs to have an understanding of instructional strategies that can be strengthened through the use of technology, along with a willingness to use these strategies; assess the effectiveness of these strategies in a particular classroom, unit, or lesson; and adjust to better meet the needs of students.

EXAMPLE INTERVIEW QUESTIONS ALIGNED WITH THE ISTE STANDARDS FOR COACHES

Supporting the Edtech Coach

The edtech coach is built to support teachers. There is a lot of giving, creating, problem-solving, and sharing that goes into this work, which is why it is important that coaches also receive the right types of support from their school and district administration. The support provided to the coach should not be entirely different from what the coach is providing for teachers.

In chapter 8, I shared two documents for reflection for edtech coaches. The first was the ISTE Standards for Coaches self-evaluation sheet. This document is meant to provide edtech coaches a way to refocus on the ISTE Standards for Coaches and provide them a space for thinking through where they currently land with their implementation of these standards in their role. The second document is the edtech coaching reflection document. This allows the coach to reflect on strengths for each of the four areas of the edtech coaching role and identifies the goal(s) the coach would like to work on to better meet the ISTE Standards. As an administrator, providing your coach the space

Example Interview Questions Aligned with the ISTE Standards for Coaches

Basic Questions to Ask:

Tell us a little bit about yourself and why you are interested in being the educational technology coach at _____ (school).

Change Agent:

If we walked into a classroom where technology was authentically integrated to enhance learning, what are some things we would or should see?

Connected Learner:

Describe how you keep yourself up-to-date on the latest instructional strategies and resources.

Collaborator:

What would your first steps be to build relationships with teachers at _____ (school)?

The educational technology coach will be asked to provide coaching cycles for teachers. With that in mind, how comfortable are you giving feedback to others and what strategies might you use to provide feedback that is useful and not overwhelming?

Learning Designer:

Describe a collaborative unit or lesson that you have designed with another educator, the process you used to design that lesson, and how you evaluated the effectiveness of the lesson.

Professional Learning Facilitator:

One of the roles of the edtech coach is to provide professional learning for teachers. How would you evaluate teacher needs when planning, and how would you structure these opportunities for your teachers?

Data-Driven Decision-Maker:

Describe how you will help support teachers in the use of data to inform instruction.

Digital Citizen Advocate:

What types of digital citizenship lessons do you believe should be taught in _____ (high school, middle school, elementary school), and how can these lessons be integrated into the curriculum?

needed for this type of reflection to take place is essential. If you are the one who runs the PLC for a group of edtech coaches, consider doing this in one of your meetings. If you are not the one who runs the PLC, simply let your coach know that it is okay to block out time to sit quietly and do this reflection alone.

Once the coaches have identified a goal or goals for the year, it is important that you, as the administrator, support them in their professional learning. There are many forms that this can take, and it does not always have to be financial support. You can support their need for professional learning by helping them carve out time in their schedule to focus on their learning and making it clear that you are okay with that time being used out for this. In the last chapter, I gave edtech coaches a revised professional-learning planning document. Working through the creation of this with your coach is one way to make sure everyone is aware of the plan and the timing needed to complete the tasks listed, ensuring that the coach is not taking on too much at one time.

You can also support coaches by providing a coaching cycle for them. This is a practice that I have taken on with my coaches, and while the dynamic may be a little different than what a coach has with a teacher (because I also provide evaluations), it is still something that has been effective for my team. I use the same coaching cycle document they use with teachers, and I only complete cycles with individuals who opt in to it. For those who have been an edtech coach or who have worked in the edtech or coaching realms before (and their focus is to work with these coaches), this may be easier to do. For administrators who are not familiar with the edtech coaching role and are not comfortable with providing coaching cycles to their coach, you could also allow for the coach from another school to come in for coaching cycles, or you could find an individual who understands coaching cycles and can provide this support for your coach, if that is something of interest.

Evaluations

While most states have an evaluation system in place, not every state has an evaluation that is focused on the edtech coaching role. If you don't have one, or if you want to add a focus on the ISTE Standards for Coaches as a way to provide data for your evaluations, you can use the ISTE Standards for Coaches evaluation sheet in Table 9.1. Notice that it is very similar to the one used by coaches for self-assessment. This can provide common talking points as you work with your edtech coach toward growth.

EDTECH COACH
EVALUATION SHEET

The rating terms are:

- **Leads Others:** The coach does this above and beyond expectations and is seen as a leader to others in this area. This may mean the coach is the go-to person for the PLC, provides PD to other coaches, or has written on the topic for publication.

- **Exceptional:** The coach does this above and beyond expectations.

- **Proficient:** The coach does this well, meeting expectations.

- **Needs Improvement:** The coach isn't meeting this standard as expected.

- **Not Applicable:** The coach cannot meet this standard in the current environment. (There may be hurdles that need to be addressed before the coach is expected to meet this standard.)

The feedback section asks for:

- **Strengths:** This box provides an opportunity for you to highlight the positives that you have noticed in your edtech coach's work.

- **Notes to Consider:** This box is intended to provide you with a place to give your coach some notes for areas of improvement.

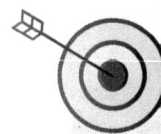

GIVING COACHES COLLABORATIVE TIME

Nichole Allmann, Technology Integration Specialist

"The most valuable resource that all teachers have is each other. Without collaboration, our growth is limited to our own perspectives" (Robert John Meehan, educator and author).

Here in Richland School District Two, located in Columbia, South Carolina, we are blessed to have a technology and learning coach (TLC) at each of our thirty-four schools. Their primary role is to work with staff to integrate technology into the curriculum in a way that develops skills, increases understanding, and explores applications that enable students and staff to utilize technology. Just as educators continue to deepen their knowledge and expertise in the classroom, we provide opportunities for our coaches to engage in continuous learning to deepen their professional knowledge and skills when it comes to instruction, technology, and adult learners.

As adult learners, we have different needs and learning styles than our students. If you were to Google the term "andragogy," you would see that there is much research around the characteristics, qualities, and needs of adult learners. Adults are more self-directed, need to know the importance and relevance of what they are learning, and draw upon their own experiences as a resource in their learning. Though these are just a few of the characteristics of adult learners, I draw on these particular qualities a bit more as a coach to our TLCs. It empowered the technology integration specialist team (the district-level coaches) to develop time for our TLCs to learn from one another, share perspectives and experiences, solve problems, make decisions, and work with each other.

Collaborative learning time has developed over the course of years. We began by devoting time in our meetings for TLCs to collaborate with one another on what they needed at the time, whether it was developing professional development together that can then be implemented at their own schools, learning a new program that was purchased for the district, or brainstorming instructional strategies around a common trend they noticed in their schools. We have implemented PLCs, where the groups determined a problem of practice and, for the year, researched, prototyped, and worked toward actionable results.

Now, with the unprecedented times we have in education, this collaborative learning time has developed into a much greater need. Our teachers were confronted with an entirely different way of teaching: completely virtual. Our TLCs have never even taught in this manner, and in order to meet the needs of our teachers, our coaches needed one another to learn, solve problems, and plan so they could effectively support their teachers. We now call this the "TLC Huddle," a time we spend together in small groups to set goals for our time together and devote our time and energy based on a current trend we are seeing.

As a district team of technology integration specialists (TISs), we knew that we wanted to provide time for our TLCs to discuss issues and challenges that were occurring at the moment. We did not want our TLCs to feel isolated during this time, like they had to have all the answers to eLearning or dual modality instruction. Having all thirty-four TLCs would not be effective; the group is too large, not all voices may be heard, and we may not be able to make as much progress as we could in a smaller group setting. Therefore, groups were created based on level: elementary and secondary levels, with elementary broken up into two groups to have smaller sizes.

There are about ten to twelve TLCs working with one TIS. As a small group, we agreed to meet once a week and individually add to the agenda prior to our huddle time because this was a time for them to engage in conversations, find answers for challenges they were having or seeing, and explore each other's perspectives as a resource. Coaches need this time to engage in dialogue and effectively work with one another in order to successfully help our teachers. It is offering a time for our coaches to develop a plan of action and next steps as a group, based on the challenge at hand. It is theirs, not an idea or strategy that was told to them to execute.

There is little buy-in when it is someone else's vision or idea that has to be done. It has to be our own, just like when our coaches are working with teachers.

As our coaches work with teachers in a planning session, they ask questions or use STEM to prompt teachers to think deeper about the goal of the lesson. It is a strategic way to allow teachers to develop their own ideas, empowering them to think on a larger scale.

TABLE 9.1 ISTE Standards for Coaches Coach Evaluation Sheet

CHANGE AGENT. Coaches inspire educators and leaders to use technology to create equitable and ongoing access to high-quality learning.

COACHES:	LEADS OTHERS	EXCEPTIONAL	PROFICIENT	NEEDS IMPROVEMENT	NOT APPLICABLE
a. Create a shared vision and culture for using technology to learn and accelerate transformation through the coaching process.					
b. Facilitate equitable use of digital learning tools and content that meet the needs of each learner.					
c. Cultivate a supportive coaching culture that encourages educators and leaders to achieve a shared vision and individual goals.					
d. Recognize educators across the organization who use technology effectively to enable high-impact teaching and learning.					
e. Connect leaders, educators, instructional support, technical support, domain experts, and solution providers to maximize the potential of technology for learning.					

Describe your rationale for the ratings chosen above:

CONNECTED LEARNER. Coaches model the ISTE Standards for Students and the ISTE Standards for Educators and identify ways to improve their coaching practice.

COACHES:	LEADS OTHERS	EXCEPTIONAL	PROFICIENT	NEEDS IMPROVEMENT	NOT APPLICABLE
a. Pursue professional learning that deepens expertise in the ISTE Standards in order to serve as a model for educators and leaders.					

b. Actively participate in professional learning networks to enhance coaching practice and keep current with emerging technology and innovations in pedagogy and the learning sciences.

c. Establish shared goals with educators, reflect on successes, and continually improve coaching and teaching practice.

Describe your rationale for the ratings chosen above:

COLLABORATOR. Coaches establish productive relationships with educators in order to improve instructional practice and learning outcomes.

COACHES:	LEADS OTHERS	EXCEPTIONAL	PROFICIENT	NEEDS IMPROVEMENT	NOT APPLICABLE
a. Establish trusting and respectful coaching relationships that encourage educators to explore new instructional strategies.					
b. Partner with educators to identify digital learning content that is culturally relevant, developmentally appropriate, and aligned to content standards.					
c. Partner with educators to evaluate the efficacy of digital learning content and tools to inform procurement decisions and adoption.					
d. Personalize support for educators by planning and modeling the effective use of technology to improve student learning.					

Describe your rationale for the ratings chosen above:

continued

LEARNING DESIGNER. Coaches model and support educators to design learning experiences and environments to meet the needs and interests of all students.

COACHES:	LEADS OTHERS	EXCEPTIONAL	PROFICIENT	NEEDS IMPROVEMENT	NOT APPLICABLE
a. Collaborate with educators to develop authentic, active learning experiences that foster student agency, deepen content mastery, and allow students to demonstrate their competency.					
b. Help educators use digital tools to create effective assessments that provide timely feedback and support personalized learning.					
c. Collaborate with educators to design accessible and active digital-learning environments that accommodate learner variability.					
d. Model the use of instructional design principles with educators to create effective digital-learning environments.					

Describe your rationale for the ratings chosen above:

PROFESSIONAL LEARNING FACILITATOR. Coaches plan, provide, and evaluate the impact of professional learning for educators and leaders to use technology to advance teaching and learning.

COACHES:	LEADS OTHERS	EXCEPTIONAL	PROFICIENT	NEEDS IMPROVEMENT	NOT APPLICABLE
a. Design professional learning based on needs assessments and frameworks for working with adults to support their cultural, social-emotional, and learning needs.					
b. Build the capacity of educators, leaders, and instructional teams to put the ISTE Standards into practice by facilitating active learning and providing meaningful feedback.					
c. Evaluate impact of professional learning and continually make improvements in order to meet school-wide vision for using technology for high-impact teaching and learning.					

Describe your rationale for the ratings chosen above:

DATA-DRIVEN DECISION-MAKER. Coaches model and support the use of qualitative and quantitative data to inform their own instruction and professional learning.

COACHES:	LEADS OTHERS	EXCEPTIONAL	PROFICIENT	NEEDS IMPROVEMENT	NOT APPLICABLE
a. Assist educators and leaders in securely collecting and analyzing student data.					
b. Support educators to interpret qualitative and quantitative data to inform their decisions and support individual student learning.					
c. Partner with educators to empower students to use learning data to set their own goals and measure their progress.					

Describe your rationale for the ratings chosen above:

DIGITAL CITIZEN ADVOCATE. Coaches model digital citizenship and support educators and students in recognizing the responsibilities and opportunities inherent in living in a digital world.

COACHES:	LEADS OTHERS	EXCEPTIONAL	PROFICIENT	NEEDS IMPROVEMENT	NOT APPLICABLE
a. Inspire and encourage educators and students to use technology for civic engagement and to address challenges to improve their communities.					
b. Partner with educators, leaders, students, and families to foster a culture of respectful online interactions and a healthy balance in their use of technology.					
c. Support educators and students to critically examine the sources of online media and identify underlying assumptions.					
d. Empower educators, leaders, and students to make informed decisions to protect their personal data and curate the digital profile they intend to reflect.					

Describe your rationale for the ratings chosen above:

continued

FEEDBACK	
Successes:	Notes to consider:

Shared Evaluations

In my current position as a technology director, my edtech coaches were traditionally only observed and evaluated by their school-based administration. The problem was that the rubric, standards, and expectations of this one role were vastly different from every other role the school administration had to evaluate. To support coaches and the school administration, I requested that of the three evaluations provided to the edtech coach, I would be responsible for one. This allowed two main things to happen:

1. The coaches' district responsibilities, projects, and activities were better able to be a part of their evaluation cycle.

2. The school administration and I were able to collaborate on the vision for the edtech coaches at their school, leaving me a better understanding of their school-based needs.

Our edtech coaches traditionally have three observations in our state. This gives the school administration two of those observations, leaving me with one for each of my coaches. This one observation also provides me the chance to have a deeper conversation with each of my coaches during their follow-up meeting. These observations have provided me with the ability to adjust the district professional learning to better meet the needs of my coaches, allowed me to offer and provide additional coaching cycles to my coaches, and given me a clearer picture of what is happening in their work. Without this opportunity, and without the coaching cycles between those observations, I am certain there would be coaches whom I would never be able to catch in the act of providing PD or co-teaching a lesson—not because they are not doing it, but because I would never know the right moment to show up at that particular building.

Hiring and Supporting the Edtech Coach Checklist

- [ ] Create a clear job description:
    - [ ] Align it with the ISTE Standards for Coaches.
    - [ ] Share it with all stakeholders.
- [ ] Provide support to your coaches:
    - [ ] Ask coaches to reflect on their role.
    - [ ] Develop a professional learning plan with the coaches.
    - [ ] Provide time and space for professional learning.
- [ ] Evaluate with the job description and ISTE Standards for Coaches in mind.

CONCLUSION: A CALL TO ACTION

The educational technology coach is a role that has been identified as a need in K–12 education and has been implemented in many schools and districts across the country. Unfortunately, this role has not been standardized in the way it is funded, implemented, or supported in schools.

Why Set Up an Edtech Coach to Focus on Instruction?

With the quick transition from "traditional" education to remote learning during the COVID-19 pandemic, teachers who may not have utilized technology before were forced to learn—and learn quickly. Teachers around the world stepped up to the plate and delivered instruction in ways they had never thought they would. They have been flexible with the requirements placed on them and worked hard to make sure they delivered the best instruction they could for their students.

Edtech coaches from across the country came out and supported teachers not just in their own schools, but through videos, podcasts, and social media, offering ideas, strategies, and resources. But imagine the growth and innovation that could take place with the same teachers who rose to the occasion during this pandemic—the teachers who did their own research, watched those videos, listened to those podcasts, and rummaged through those digital resources to create an online learning experience for their students.

Imagine if those same teachers were partnered with an edtech coach at their own school, setting their own goals, co-planning, co-teaching, and receiving feedback and personalized support from a coach they work with on a daily basis. The power in this type of collaboration could prove to be a catalyst that helps us to change K–12 education in a way that makes learning student-centered and engaging.

The edtech coaching role should not be something that is in place only where it can be afforded. It should be in place in *every* school, in *every* district, in *every* state across the country. If we are willing to fund technology for our staff and students, we have to be willing to fund the support that teachers need to implement that technology effectively.

A NEED FOR CONSISTENCY

Dr. Vanessa Wrenn, North Carolina Department of Public Instruction Director of Digital Teaching and Learning

Quality instruction, no matter the instructional model or delivery format, always begins and ends with the teacher. Not unlike any other industry—healthcare, finance, or construction—an artisan workforce equipped with cutting-edge technologies is the most important factor to quality outcomes and advancement. So it should come as no surprise that the education industry is no different: artisan teachers must be skilled in educational technologies to gain quality outcomes and provide a rewarding learning experience for all students. Sustained coaching for quality educational technology practice is one of the most critical factors in providing access to quality learning.

Educational technology (edtech) coaches are the critical component to reach high levels of effective technology practices. Edtech coaches help teachers integrate technology resources and strategies in their instruction in ways that advance student learning and ensure that the learning process provides engagement and relevancy. Edtech coaches promote a shared vision that transforms teaching, building operations, and the culture of schools. District- and school-based edtech coaches are familiar with the district's goal and priorities. They know and understand their teachers' and students' abilities.

Currently, the use of edtech coaches and teachers' access to an edtech coach is indiscriminate. Edtech coaches are often used as computer technicians, especially in environments where each student is assigned a computer. Often, when a district goes 1:1, the immediate strain on the technology staff is supplemented with the edtech coaching staff. Although we have edtech coaching standards, we do not have a standardized approach to funding edtech coach positions. While we fund teaching positions based on student enrollment, in many states we do not allocate state-funded positions for edtech coaches.

Additionally, we do not have a standardized ratio of edtech coaches per student as we do for other teaching and support staff. Therefore, districts are left on their own to fund edtech coaches locally or to pull from existing teacher position allotments. This often creates an environment where sustained coaching is haphazard and does not create equitable access. The COVID-19 pandemic has pulled back the curtain to reveal the inequities in access to edtech coaching and digital resources. All research and practical experience show us that providing ongoing embedded coaching support, which is collaborative, helps teachers to grow, take risks, and embrace the vision needed to create a student-centered school culture. As a nation, we must work to mitigate the digital divide, and that work must include equitable access to edtech coaches.

APPENDIX: PLANNING AND SCHEDULING TEMPLATES

Plan for School Goal with Singular Focus

GOAL:

SESSIONS MEET: **SESSION LENGTH:**

DATE	SESSION TITLE	SESSION DESCRIPTION	SESSION MATERIALS	PREWORK
AUG.				
SEPT.				
OCT.				
NOV.				
DEC.				
JAN.				
FEB.				
MAR.				
APR.				
MAY				

Planning Professional Learning for PLC Goal

GOAL:

SESSIONS MEET: **SESSION LENGTH:**

DATE	SESSION TITLE	SESSION DESCRIPTION
AUG.		
SEPT.		
OCT.		
NOV.		
DEC.		
JAN.		
FEB.		
MAR.		
APR.		
MAY		

SESSION FORMAT	SESSION MATERIALS	PREWORK

Professional Learning Session Request Form

GOAL:

SESSIONS MEET: **SESSION LENGTH:**

SESSIONS	SESSION DESCRIPTIONS	DATE REQUESTED

Sample Planning Chart for Individual Goal through Choice

	GOAL 1	GOAL 2	GOAL 3	GOAL 4
AUG.				
SEPT.				
OCT.				
NOV.				
DEC.				
JAN.				
FEB.				
MAR.				
APR.				
MAY				

References

Aguilar, E. (2013). *The art of coaching: Effective strategies for school transformation*. San Francisco, CA: Wiley.

Bakhshaei, M., Hardy, A., Francisco, A., Noakes, S., & Fusco, J. (2018). *Fostering powerful use of technology through instructional coaching*. Digital Promise. https://digitalpromise.org/wp-content/uploads/2018/08/DLP_CoachingReport_2018.pdf

Campbell, P. & Malkus, N. (2011). The impact of elementary mathematics coaches on student achievement. *The Elementary School Journal, 111*(3), 430-454. https://doi.org/10.1086/657654

Darling-Hammond, L., Hyler, M. E., & Gardner, M. (2017). *Effective teacher professional development* (research brief). Learning Policy Institute. https://learningpolicyinstitute.org/product/effective-teacher-professional-development-report

Gabriel, J. G., & Farmer, P. C. (2009). *How to help your school thrive without breaking the bank*. Association for Supervision and Curriculum Development.

Inan, F.A., & Lowther, D.L. (2010). Factors affecting technology integration in K-12 classrooms: a path model. *Educational Technology Research and Development, 58*(2), 137–154. https://doi.org/10.1007/s11423-009-9132-y

International Society for Technology in Education. (2019). ISTE standards for coaches. https://www.iste.org/standards/for-coaches

Kane, B. D., & Rosenquist, B. (2018, April). "Making the most of instructional coaches: Although coaching shows promise for professional development, some instructional coaches are spread too thin to focus on instruction." *Phi Delta Kappan, 99*(7), 21. https://kappanonline.org/kane-instructional-coaches/

Knight, J. (2018). *The impact cycle: What instructional coaches should do to foster powerful improvements in teaching*. Thousand Oaks, CA: Corwin.

Kolb, L. (2017). *Learning first, technology second: The educator's guide to designing authentic lessons*. International Society for Technology in Education.

Kraft, M., & Blazar, D. (2018). "Taking teacher coaching to scale: Can personalized training become standard practice?" *Education Next, 18*(4). https://link.gale.com/apps/doc/A556890659/OVIC?u=lom_accessmich&sid=OVIC&xid=2fa3e60e

Killion, J. J. (2017). Meta-analysis reveals coaching's positive impact on instruction and achievement. *Learning Professional, 38*(2), 20-23. http://mathleadership.org/wp-content/uploads/2018/01/Meta-analysis-reveals-coaching%E2%80%99s-positive-impact-on-instruction-and-achievement.pdf

Liu, F., Ritzhaupt, A. D., Dawson, K., & Barron, A. E. (2017). "Explaining technology integration in K–12 classrooms: A multilevel path analysis model." *Educational Technology, Research and Development, 65*(4), 795-813. https://doi.org/10.1007/s11423-016-9487-9

Love, N. (2008). *The data coach's guide to improving learning for all students: Unleashing the power of collaborative inquiry*. Thousand Oaks, CA: Corwin Press.

Matherson, L., & Windle, T. (2017). "What do teachers want from their professional development? Four emerging themes." *Delta Kappa Gamma Bulletin, 83*(3), 28-32. https://www.dkg.org/DKGDocs/2017_Jour_83-3_Systems-to-Address-Quality-Teaching.pdf.

McBride, A., & Dirkin, K. (2020). "Evaluation of a digital teaching and learning professional development program: Not a revolution, but an evolution." In D. Schmidt-Crawford (Ed.), *Proceedings of Society for Information Technology & Teacher Education International Conference*, 457-463. https://www.learntechlib.org/primary/p/215782/

Meeuwse, K. & Mason, D. (2018). *Personalized professional learning for educators*. Hershey, PA: IGI Global.

North Carolina State University. North Carolina Digital Learning Initiative. (n.d.). https://ncdli.fi.ncsu.edu/rubric/index.html

Rolfe, G., Freshwater, D., Jasper, M. (2001) Critical reflection in nursing and the helping professions: a user's guide. Basingstoke: Palgrave Macmillan.

Showers, B., & Joyce, B. (1996). "The evolution of peer coaching." *Educational Leadership, 53*, 12-16. http://educationalleader.com/subtopicintro/read/ASCD/ASCD_351_1.pdf

Toll, C. A. (2018). *Educational coaching: A partnership for problem-solving*. Alexandria, VA: ASCD.

University of Minnesota. Active Learning. (n.d.). https://cei.umn.edu/active-learning

Index

A
ABLE system, 38
action plans, 69
active learning strategies, 35, 37
adjustments, making, 37–38, 47
advertising, 82
affective model, 15, 16
agendas, sample
   co-planning meeting, 45
   post-observation, 68
Aguilar, Elena, 15
Allmann, Nichole, 104–105
Avengers: Infinity War, 52

B
behavioral model, 15, 16
Bennett, Channing, 4
body systems, teaching, 52
brainstorming, 47, 69, 78

C
calendars, 85, 86
change, bringing about, 4
Change Agent role
   interview questions, 101
   performance evaluation, 106
   self-evaluation, 90
choice, embedding
   resources, when to engage with, 33–34
   resources, which to engage with, 34
   tools, 34–35
classroom, modeling in, 48–49
coaching cycles, formal
   about, 13–14, 56–57
   action plan, creating, 69
   administrator use with coaches, 102
   agenda, sample post-observation, 68
   checklist, 71
   dynamic learning project, 61
   edtech coaching cycle, 62–70
   goal-setting, 65, 69
   Impact Cycle, 60–61
   implement and support phase, 69–70
   initiate phase, 62–65
   observation phase, 65–66
   participants, getting right, 63
   plan phase, 68–69
   problem-solving cycle, 57, 60
   reflection, 66–67
   support plan, creating, 69
   "teacher talks it out," 68
   timeline for next observation, 69
   timing of, 70
   transition to, 58–59

types, 57–61
"what I heard and saw," 68
what-ifs, 69
coaching menu, 82
collaborative learning time, 104–105
collaborative model, 15, 16
Collaborator role
    interview questions, 101
    performance evaluation, 107
    self-evaluation, 91
Connected Learner role
    interview questions, 101
    performance evaluation, 106–107
    self-evaluation, 90–91
co-planning
    about, 42–43
    agenda, sample, 45
    drafting plan, 47
    follow-up after meeting, 47–48
    goals, defining, 46
    next steps, planning, 47
    preparation before meeting, 43–44
    process during meeting, 44–47, 52
    questions to ask, 43–44
    success and struggle points, 46
    "teacher talks it out," 46
    walkthrough and adjust, 47
    "what I heard," 46
    what-ifs, 47
co-teaching, 51
COVID-19 pandemic, 2, 8, 84, 85, 113

D

data analysis and usage, 52–54
The Data Coach's Guide to Improving Learning for All Students (Love), 53
Data-Driven Decision-Maker role
    interview questions, 101
    performance evaluation, 108
    self-evaluation, 93
decision tree, technical support, 83
dialogical coaching, 15
differentiated learning goals for students, 23–26, 28–29
Digital Citizen Advocate role
    interview questions, 101
    performance evaluation, 108
    self-evaluation, 94
digital citizenship, modeling, 50–51
digital learning coaches. *See* edtech coaches
Digital Promise coaching model, 61
directive coaching, 15
district goals, 22, 23
drafting plans, 47
dynamic learning project, 61

E

edtech coaches
    benefits of, 4–5
    evaluating, 103, 106–110
    hiring/assigning, 8, 100, 101
    interview questions, 101
    job descriptions, 99
    learning time for, 104–105
    licensing of, 5

edtech coaches (continued)
   names for, 5
   professional learning by, 96-97, 102
   role of, 5-7, 11-16
   supporting, 100, 102
   teachers, relationship with, 40-41
edtech coaching cycle
   implement and support phase, 69-70
   initiate phase, 62-65
   observation phase, 65-66
   plan phase, 68-69
   reflection, 66-67
Educational Coaching (Toll), 16
eLearning coaches. *See* edtech coaches
evaluating edtech coaches, 103, 106-110

F

facilitative coaching, 15
Farmer, Paul C., 11
feedback, 37-38, 79-80
focused leadership responsibilities. *See* leadership responsibilities, focused
Foltos, Les, 58
formal coaching cycles. *See* coaching cycles, formal
forms
   educational technology coaching interest, 63
   educational technology coaching observation, 66
   ISTE Standards for Coaches coach evaluation sheet, 106-110
   professional learning plan, 96
   professional learning session planning, 25-26
   project feedback, 80
   project plan brainstorm, 78

   project spreadsheet, 79
   reflection, 95
   reflection protocol, 67
   session planning sheet, 32
   technical support decision tree, 83

G

Gabriel, John G., 11
goals
   coaching models with, 15
   defining, 46
   district, 22, 23
   individual, 30-31
   professional learning, 20-31
   professional learning community, 27-29
   restating, 69
   school, 22-26
   setting, 20-21, 65, 69
   vision and, 20-21
groups, small, 32-33

H

hiring/assigning edtech coaches, 8, 100, 101
How to Help Your School Thrive without Breaking the Bank (Gabriel & Farmer), 11

I

identifying the work, 76-77
Impact Cycle, 60-61
implement and support phase, 69-70
individual goals, 30-31
initiate phase, 62-65
instructional technology facilitators. *See* edtech coaches

intellectual model, 15, 16
interview questions for edtech coach applicants, 101
ISTE Standards for Coaches
   about, 10
   coach evaluation sheet, 103, 106–110
   interview questions aligned with, 101
   self-evaluation, 90–94
ISTE Standards for Educators, 49
ISTE Standards for Students, 49

J
job descriptions, 99

K
King, Holly, 74–75
Knight, Jim, 15, 60
Kolb, Liz, 20

L
leadership niche, 73
leadership responsibilities, focused
   about, 14, 72
   checklist, 80
   feedback, gathering, 79–80
   leadership niche, finding, 73
   projects and programs, 73–76
   work, identifying, 76–77
   work, organizing, 77–79
Learning Designer role
   interview questions, 101
   performance evaluation, 108
   self-evaluation, 92
Learning First, Technology Second (Kolb), 20

Learning Policy Institute, 3
learning time for edtech coaches, 104–105
licensing of edtech coaches, 5

M
menu, coaching, 82
modeling
   about, 36
   in classroom alongside students, 48–49
   of digital citizenship, 50–51
   in professional learning sessions, 50

N
names for edtech coaches, 5
next steps, planning, 47
North Carolina Digital Learning Progress Rubric, 22–23

O
observation phase, 65–66
Ohio ABLE system, 38
organizing the work, 77–79

P
participants, getting right, 63
pedagogy-focused professional learning, 20
Peer Coaching (Foltos), 58
performance evaluations, 103, 106–110
personalized teacher support. *See* teacher support, personalized
plan phase, 68–69
PLCs (professional learning communities), 27–29, 79
Porter, Nikita, 58–59

priorities and support services, advertising, 82
problem-solving cycle, 57, 60
professional learning
  about, 12–13
  active learning strategies, 35, 37
  adjusting plans, 37–38
  benefits of, 18
  checklist, 39
  choice, embedding, 33–35
  for coaches, 96–97, 102
  delivery formats, 18–19
  district goals and, 22, 23
  feedback, 37–38
  goals of, 20–31
  importance of, 17–18
  individual goals and, 30–31
  modeling, 50
  pedagogy-focused, 20
  professional learning community goals and, 27–29
  qualities within sessions, 31–38
  research on, 3
  resources, choices about, 33–34
  scheduling, 19
  school goals and, 22–26
  session planning sheet, 32
  small groups in, 32–33
  time considerations, 35
  tools, choice of, 34–35
  vision and goals, 20–21
professional learning communities (PLCs), 27–29, 79

Professional Learning Facilitator role
  interview questions, 101
  performance evaluation, 108
  self-evaluation, 92–93
project management, 77–79
project spreadsheet, 79
projects and programs, 73–76

R

reflection, 66–67, 100, 102
research, 3, 41–42
resources, choices about, 33–34
rhythm of school, 84–85
Richland School District Two (Columbia, SC), 104–105

S

scheduling
  observation, 69
  professional learning, 19
  sit-and-do tasks, 86
  transparency about, 85
school goals, 22–26
school rhythm, 84–85
science teachers, 52
self-evaluation
  about, 88–89
  ISTE Standards for Coaches, 90–94
  reflection form, 95
shared evaluations, 110
Shreffler, Brad, 36
Sirkin, Marsha, 6–7

small groups, 32–33
spreadsheet example, project, 79
students, differentiated learning goals for, 23–26, 28–29
success and struggle points, 46
support, personalized teacher. *See* teacher support, personalized
support plans, 69
supporting edtech coaches, 100, 102

T

teacher support, personalized
   about, 13
   checklist, 55
   co-planning, 42–48, 52
   co-teaching, 51
   data analysis and usage, 52–54
   modeling, 48–51
   relationship, teacher-coach, 40–41
   research, 41–42
"teacher talks it out," 46, 68
teachers. *See also* teacher support, personalized
   coaches, relationship with, 40–41
   modeling with, 36
   roles and responsibilities, 1–2

technical support, 83–84
technology integration specialists. *See* edtech coaches
ten-minute rule, 83–84
Toll, Cathy A., 15–16, 57
tools, choice about, 34–35
transformational coaching, 15

V

vision, 11–12, 20–21

W

walkthrough and adjust, 47
"what I heard," 46, 68
what-ifs, 47, 69
Wolf, Connie, 52
work
   identifying, 76–77
   organizing, 77–79

Your opinion matters
Tell us how we're doing!

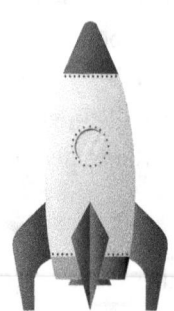

Your feedback helps ISTE create the best possible resources for teaching and learning in the digital age. Share your thoughts with the community or tell us how we're doing!

You can:

- Write a review at amazon.com or barnesandnoble.com.
- Mention this book on social media and follow ISTE on Twitter @iste, Facebook @ISTEconnects or Instagram @isteconnects
- Email us at books@iste.org with your questions or comments.